Psychology and Religion within an Ideological Surround

Religion and Psychology

Editor-in-Chief

Ralph W. Hood, Jr. (*University of Tennessee at Chattanooga, USA*)

Associate Editors

Mohammad Khodayari fard (*University of Tehran, Iran*)
Tomas Lindgren (*Umeå Universitet, Sweden*)
Tatjana Schnell (*Universität Innsbruck, Austria*)
Katarzyna Skrzypińska (*University of Gdańsk, Poland*)
W. Paul Williamson (*Henderson State University, Arkadelphia, USA*)

Volumes published in the Brill Research Perspectives title are listed at *brill.com/rpsy*

Psychology and Religion within an Ideological Surround

By

Paul J. Watson

BRILL

LEIDEN | BOSTON

This paperback book edition is simultaneously published as issue 1.1 (2019) of *Religion and Psychology*, DOI:10.1163/25897128-12340001.

Library of Congress Control Number: 2019942152

Typeface for the Latin, Greek, and Cyrillic scripts: "Brill". See and download: brill.com/brill-typeface.

ISBN 978-90-04-41118-0 (paperback)
ISBN 978-90-04-41120-3 (e-book)

Copyright 2019 by Paul J. Watson. Published by Koninklijke Brill NV, Leiden, The Netherlands.
Koninklijke Brill NV incorporates the imprints Brill, Brill Hes & De Graaf, Brill Nijhoff, Brill Rodopi, Brill Sense, Hotei Publishing, mentis Verlag, Verlag Ferdinand Schöningh and Wilhelm Fink Verlag.
Koninklijke Brill NV reserves the right to protect the publication against unauthorized use and to authorize dissemination by means of offprints, legitimate photocopies, microform editions, reprints, translations, and secondary information sources, such as abstracting and indexing services including databases. Requests for commercial re-use, use of parts of the publication, and/or translations must be addressed to Koninklijke Brill NV.

This book is printed on acid-free paper and produced in a sustainable manner.

Contents

In Memoriam: Paul J. Watson (June 23, 1948–March 10, 2019)   1
Psychology and Religion within an Ideological Surround   2
  Paul J. Watson
 Abstract   2
 Keywords   2
 1 Introduction   2
  1.1 *Complexity of Rationalities*   3
  1.2 *Tentativeness*   5
 2 Psychology, Religion, and Social Rationalities   5
  2.1 *Religion and the Methodological Atheism of Psychology*   6
  2.2 *Critique of Modernism*   8
  2.3 *Social Rationality, Ideology, and Incommensurability*   11
  2.4 *Future Objectivity and Post-postmodernism*   14
  2.5 *Post-postmodern Dialogue and Triumphalisms*   19
  2.6 *Conclusion*   21
 3 Empiricism, Dialogue, and the Operationalization of Religious Traditions   22
  3.1 *ISM and Empiricism as Ideological*   23
  3.2 *Operationalizing Traditions and Dialogue*   26
  3.3 *Sin and Grace within a Christian Ideological Surround*   27
  3.4 *Muslim Experiential Religiousness in Iran*   29
  3.5 *Greater Jihad in Pakistan*   33
  3.6 *Broader Conclusions about the Operationalization of Traditions*   37
  3.7 *Resistances*   40
 4 Theist Methodological Dialogism   40
  4.1 *Psychometric Deconstruction of Psychometrics*   41
  4.2 *Direct Rational Analysis*   42
  4.3 *Correlational Marker Analysis*   43
  4.4 *Comparative Rationality Analysis*   44
  4.5 *Empirical Translation Schemes*   47
  4.6 *Statistical Controls for Ideology*   49
  4.7 *Conclusions*   51
 5 Religious Openness Hypothesis   52
  5.1 *Faith and Intellect Oriented Reflection*   53
  5.2 *Fundamentalism outside the West*   55
  5.3 *Christian Religious Xenophilia*   57
  5.4 *Methodological Theism as Necessary for 'Objectivity'*   62

6　Dialogue and Trans-rationality　64
　　6.1　*"I dialogue; therefore, I am"*　65
　　6.2　*Private Rationality: "I reflect; therefore, I am"*　65
　　6.3　*Communal Rationality: "I agree; therefore, I am"*　67
　　6.4　*Public Rationality: "I disagree; therefore, I am"*　69
　　6.5　*Secularization and Trans-rationality*　72
　　6.6　*In Conclusion, ISM Inconclusion*　74
Acknowledgements　76
References　78

In Memoriam
Paul J. Watson (June 23, 1948–March 10, 2019)

Not long after agreeing to write this book Paul was diagnosed with a terminal illness. It required him to retire from the University of Tennessee at Chattanooga as Emeritus Professor of Psychology where he taught for over 41 years, both in the Psychology Department as well as in the University Honors Program. Paul and I had long discussion regarding not only his illness, but the effect on his family and on the prospects for completing his book. He wisely decided to retire from the university, and to focus his remaining time on his family and the completion of this book. He wanted to present his ISM model, based upon over 30 years of research and hundreds of published articles. He was not only a scholar and researcher, but devout a Quaker, regularly worshiping at The Chattanooga Friends Meeting. He found not conflict between science and religion and was committed to fostering a dialogue not only between religions but between religions and disciplines that study them. Dialogue is an integral part of his Ideological Surround Model. This book is a fitting tribute to a scholar who sought to foster understanding between psychology and religion and who literally completed this manuscript on his deathbed.

Ralph W. Hood Jr.

Psychology and Religion within an Ideological Surround

Paul J. Watson
University of Tennessee at Chattanooga, USA

Abstract

For over three decades, an Ideological Surround Model (ISM) has pursued theoretical and methodological innovations designed to enhance the 'truth' and 'objectivity' of research into psychology and religion. The foundational argument of the ISM is that psychology as well as religion unavoidably operates within the limits of an ideological surround. Methodological theism, therefore, needs to supplement the methodological atheism that dominates the contemporary social sciences. Methodological theism should operationalize the meaningfulness of religious traditions and demonstrate empirically that the influences of ideology cannot be ignored. The ISM more generally suggests that contemporary social scientific rationalities need to be supplemented my more complex dialogical rationalities. Beliefs in secularization should also be supplemented by beliefs in trans-rationality.

Keywords

psychology – religion – ideology – dialogue – trans-rationality

1   Introduction

> More than ever, I am convinced that history has meaning and that its meaning is terrifying.
> RENÉ GIRARD (2010, p. xvii)

∴

This monograph synthesizes over three decades of research using an Ideological Surround Model (ISM) of the relationship between psychology and religion. Acts of imagination usefully describe the kinds of challenges that led to this model. Imagine you are an adolescent living in London during World War I (WWI), and your father dies at the Battle of the Somme in 1916. This single battle led to more deaths than the previous century of European warfare (Appleyard 1992). You might take some comfort from the idea that WWI was at least supposed to be "the war to end all wars." But then imagine your son dies on D-Day almost three decades later during the exponentially greater bloodshed of World War II (WWII). Finally, imagine you live long enough through the 20th Century to witness more and more death and destruction. The spectacle of Pol Pot in Cambodia, for instance, occurs toward the end of your life. Such experiences will eventually lead to a question, "How can violence cast out violence?"

Almost everyone will have at least an implicit answer to this question. Most will probably presume that violence used rationally is the only option for casting out violence. But where *is* the evidence that rational violence can ultimately eliminate violence? Recent Western incursions into Iraq supply only one data point among many that argues against the claim (see e.g., Mekhennet 2017). Other, mostly religious answers will assume that violence cannot cast out violence, which must be resisted through some form of pacifism. But where *is* the evidence that pacifism can ultimately cast out violence? Especially nonreligious skeptics will point out that refusals to use violence in a violent world will likely result in your own or in someone else's death.

Neither type of answer seems fully defensible empirically, nor are logical arguments alone likely to convince advocates of rational violence to embrace pacifism or vice versa. Moreover, all this occurs in a world that creates increasingly efficient technologies of death. Nuclear warfare, for example, can now exterminate all humans on the planet in an alarmingly short period of time. Girard (2010) essentially argues that religions in the long history of humanity sought to control this potentially all-consuming violence but that the efficacy of those controls have long been under progressive decline. In the absence of an appropriate response to this problem, humanity seems doomed to battle to the end. The meaning of history and of violence within it turns out to be terrifying.

1.1 *Complexity of Rationalities*

As interpreted through the ISM, the issue of violence only begins to capture a central cultural problem that is also at the heart of the relationship between psychology and religion. This relationship more generally and importantly reveals that the rationalities of social life are unavoidably limited. Section 2 will make this argument by explaining why social rationalities necessarily operate within a surround of different ideological assumptions about ultimate standards and about their normative and sociological implications. Relativism across social rationalities is an undeniable empirical reality, as daily interactions among individuals of different genders, races, religions, educational levels, and occupations will, for example, make clear. The ISM maintains, however, that relativism is not and cannot be a normative reality. Instead, rationalities of religion and psychology should unite in dialogues to defend 'truth' and 'objectivity' in the face of relativism. The ISM presents a conceptual framework that explains how this could be possible.

Several points about the writing style of this monograph deserve emphasis here because they first appear in Section 2. This section will argue that three ultimate standards are especially influential in contemporary social life: God, Nature, and Power. Capitalization of those terms will designate their status as ideologically ultimate. The lack of capitals elsewhere will reflect their more straightforward usage in other contexts. In addition, words like 'truth' and 'objectivity' will sometimes be placed in quotation marks to indicate that these terms will roughly reflect common parlance but that their exact meanings will require dialogical negotiations across ideological perspectives.

Admission that the rationalities of psychology are limited in a manner similar to those of religion has important implications for the study of psychology and religion. As explained in Section 3, this realization requires a social science of methodological and metaphysical theism. Research programs dedicated to that goal will operationalize religious traditions in a way that demonstrates how they make sense empirically. Methodological theism can and also should be brought into dialogue with the methodological atheism that dominates the contemporary social sciences. Those dialogues can profoundly enhance thinking within both religious and psychological ideological surrounds.

Section 4 suggests that social scientific resistances to methodological theism may prevent beneficial dialogues from occurring. The ISM attempts to overcome such resistances through innovations that can be described as a theist methodological dialogism. The data analytic procedures of this dialogism operate as a psychometric deconstruction of psychometrics that seeks to demonstrate that the influences of ideology cannot be eliminated from research into psychology and religion. Attention to those influences can enhance the 'objectivity' of both psychology and religion.

Methodological theism makes it possible to view religion and psychology from previously underrepresented perspectives and as a consequence to discover previously unsuspected relationships. Claims that conservative religious commitments are psychologically and socially narrow-minded are well-established within the broader research literature (e.g., Altemeyer and Hunsberger 1992, 2004). Attention to ideological factors, nevertheless, can make it clear that conservative religiousness also has potentials for psychosocial openness. Section 5 reviews evidence for a Religious Openness Hypothesis that supports this conclusion cross-culturally. More generally, this line of research further illustrates the benefits of bringing theist and non-theist psychological perspectives into dialogue.

The central argument of the Section 6 will be that intersections between psychology and religion reveal a need for more complex understandings of social rationality. Rather than individualistic philosophical moorings in the 'I' of Descartes *cogito*, the contemporary social sciences and social life should find more productive foundations in the development of dialogical rationalities. Dialogical rationalities turn out to be private, communal, and public. All three are important and deserve to be understood in their own right. Public rationalities, in particular, require defense and development, or at least that is the diagnosis of the ISM. This perspective also implies that social scientific models of rationality as a process of secularization need to be supplemented by something else. That something else would be a 'trans-rationality' model.

1.2 *Tentativeness*

Ultimately, the ISM contends that social rationalities should engage in a neverending process of dialogue in which 'truth' and 'objectivity' are approached but never finally reached. The present description of the ISM may eventually prove to be inadequate and require further development through dialogue. More problematic may be the responses of some who will simply find the ISM theist framework to be worthy of reactions ranging nonchalance to contempt. Such resistances will mean that its arguments will never be read. The claim of the ISM is that all arguments deserve to be read and submitted to thoughtful dialogical consideration. Many truly crucial dialogues remain. This monograph concludes with examples of only a few of the possibilities.

2 Psychology, Religion, and Social Rationalities

Psychology and religion intersect in a cultural space that illustrates a central challenge within contemporary social life. The ISM describes this challenge as the problematic relationship that invariably exists among social rationalities within pluralistic cultures (Watson 1993, 2011). Social rationalities refer to what Taylor (2007) calls "social imaginaries" and defines as the manner in which people "imagine their social existence, how they fit together with others, how things go on between them and their fellows, the expectations which are normally met, and the deeper normative notions and images which underlie these expectations" (p. 71). Pluralistic cultures, therefore, necessarily struggle with how to accommodate the sometimes strikingly different, deeper normative notions and images that appear within their diverse social rationalities.

How psychologists imagine themselves and religious persons, for example, can differ radically from how religious persons imagine themselves and psychologists. These differences will reflect contrasting normative notions and images about which rational compromises will seem impossible for at least some psychologists and for at least some religious persons. The ISM pursues the development of a social science that responds as rationally as possible to these apparent impossibilities of rational compromise. Seeing the need for such a social science first requires a sketch of how contemporary psychology most commonly organizes its relationships with religion and vice versa.

2.1 *Religion and the Methodological Atheism of Psychology*

Dominant perspectives within the contemporary psychology of religion pursue an 'objectivity' dedicated to the reduction of traditional religion to psychological processes. Religion, in other words, must be explained by making it into something else; so, at least some religious critics might complain that the goal is to explain religion away. For many psychologists, however, the 'objectivity' of this approach will seem self-evident. Traditional religion, after all, organizes its 'psychology' around some vision of 'God.' 'God' is not open to direct empirical observation and thus can have no reality within the social sciences. Only events in nature, and never anything supra-natural, can be observed. The conclusion seems indisputable. The psychology of religion requires methodological naturalism, and methodological naturalism dictates methodological atheism. Even social scientists sympathetic to religion can see this bracketing out of 'God' as essential (e.g., Berger 1967). Many psychologists of religion, therefore, would presumably have no qualms about describing themselves as *methodological atheists*.

Reactions to methodological atheism defy exhaustive description. *Methodological agnostics* might advocate a more cautious approach in which the possibility would be accepted that 'God' could not be explained away (Porpora 2006). The interpretative challenges, nevertheless, seem daunting because the "question to be considered is whether, if the reality of supermundane objects of religious experience [i.e., 'God'] were granted, those objects could explain anything other than their own perception and, if so, would they, by their very entanglement in the mundane causal chain thereby cease being super-mundane" (Porpora, p. 73). Only *methodological and metaphysical theists* who formally refuse to explain 'God' away would seem immune to such mundane entanglements (Johnson 2007; Roberts and Watson 2010). In the absence of arguments to the contrary, therefore, any research program based upon methodological agnosticism would seem destined to collapse into methodological atheism.

Some psychologists might deny any commitment to methodological atheism and might instead describe themselves as *non-metaphysical empiricists*. They would argue that metaphysical considerations have absolutely no place within social scientific research programs, with the existence or nonexistence of 'God' being just one example. Religion merely operates as one class of variables that displays empirically interesting and sometimes practically useful linkages with other classes of variables (e.g., Batson, Shoenrade, and Ventis 1993). These psychologists will go on to argue that a metaphysically blind social science will generate brute data that will 'objectively' answer questions about religion. In their research, however, non-metaphysical empiricists will make no room for a 'God' that cannot eventually be explained by something else; so, they essentially operate as methodological atheists.

Some psychologists will be religious and will want to defend their commitments to God in a position that might be called *religious synthesis*. Religious synthesizers would find the procedures of methodological atheism useful, but they would also believe that all obtained data could be assimilated in some way within a theistic worldview (Coe and Hall 2010; Jones 2010; Myers 2010). Such an approach faces challenges from two opposite directions.

First, from a secular direction, synthesizing religious interpretations have displayed a diminished intellectual traction at least since the time of William of Ockham (c. 1285–c. 1348). Ockham argued that "there was one truth described by Christian revelation, which was beyond doubt and beyond rational comprehension, and there was another truth comprising the observable particular facts described by empirical science and rational philosophy" (Tarnas 1991, p. 205). God defined one area of understanding; reason and science defined another. In explanations of empirical phenomena, therefore, "entities are not to be multiplied beyond necessity" (Tarnas, p. 203), and for most psychologists of religion, 'God' and the conceptual apparatus of religious synthesis will be a multiplication of entities beyond necessity. Ockham's goal may have been to protect timeless faith from the changing interpretative frameworks of philosophy and science. For many, however, the result will instead be the inevitable disappearance of religion through secularization.

Second, from a religious direction, the religious psychology of synthesizers must confront challenges associated with its use of the words 'religious' and 'psychology.' A 'religious' psychology that offers theistic interpretations of methodological atheism will have limited resources within itself to assess the validity of its own interpretations. Religious worldviews used in these interpretations can differ (Sandage et al. 2017) and can contain traces of accommodations to and conflicts with the wider culture. Compromises with professional psychology, for example, may be especially obvious for at least some religious critics.

With regards to the word 'psychology,' some religious skeptics will see modern psychology as inextricably grounded in Godlessness. For these *antipsychological theists*, the methodological atheism of the discipline camouflages a metaphysical atheism that must be rejected. 'Psychology' should instead find exclusive, nonscientific moorings in the traditions and texts of faith (Powlison 2010). Given these secular and religious challenges, religious synthesis seems limited in its ability to construct an integrated and influential social rationality and seems vulnerable to schism within religious communities and to outright dismissal in the wider culture.

For at least some psychologists, these secular and religious challenges will mean that all religious perspectives will inevitably collapse sociologically into metaphysical atheism. Freud (1927/1961a) is an obvious exemplar of these *metaphysical atheists*. God, he argued, is an illusion, and by illusion, he meant a wish-fulfilment. This wish-fulfillment helps humanity handle the sense of helplessness associated with the harsh realities of life. The protection supplied by a father in childhood supplies the wishful prototype for a 'God' who supplies protection later in life and even after death. Freud believed that such illusions would never survive the discoveries of science. "You know why," he argued, "nothing can withstand reason and experience, and the contradiction which religion offers to both is all too palpable" (Freud, p. 54). Freud then took it to be axiomatic that "science is no illusion. But an illusion it would be to suppose that what science cannot give us we can get elsewhere" (Freud, p. 56). Religion must be reduced to psychology. Religion must be explained away.

2.2 *Critique of Modernism*

Freud (1927/1961a) expressed his 'objectivity' about religion within a modernist perspective that some will no longer see as unquestionably 'objective.' Prior to the modernist Enlightenment, pre-modern rationality organized social life around a Catholic vision of God, but Reformation conflicts over that vision led to the Thirty Years' War from 1618 to 1648 (Toulman 1990). The wide-spread death and destruction of this war ended with the Treaty of Westphalia, which essentially effected a divorce between Catholics and Protestants into separate nation states. No longer could a Catholic pre-modern rationality organize social life across societies.

Modernism, therefore, replaced Catholic pre-modernism. Peace seemed to require a new vocabulary that did not demand prior agreement on the definition of God and of associated religious concepts (Stout 1988). William of Ockham had stood at the origins of a *via moderna* that opposed an earlier *via antigua* (Tarnas 1991). The Enlightenment expanded the *via moderna* by focusing on the empirical science and rational philosophy that Ockham had separated from knowledge of God. After the Thirty Years' War, the expectation was that the reason and experience of both science and philosophy would supply a new master rationality for peacefully reorganizing social life.

Descartes (1637/1968) essentially offered an epistemological manifesto for this master rationality. He spelled out four steps of method that began with a programmatic process of doubting in which an individual "was never to accept anything as true" that did not appear "to be self-evidently so" (Descartes, p. 41). After this skepticism, reductionism would come as a second step in which the objects of experience would be subdivided into constituent parts sufficiently small so that no disagreements could exist in how they were observed. Then, reason would begin with the smallest constituent parts to inductively reconstruct a perception of the whole now objectively refined by skepticism. The rationalism of the fourth step would evaluate the ongoing and overall final process to guarantee its logical sufficiency. For Freud and for modernists more generally, the reason and experience of this Cartesian science seemed to promise an objectivity that would be indubitable to anyone relying upon their "pure natural reason" (Descartes, p. 91).

Cultural developments eventually cast doubt upon this modernist epistemological certainty. A first thing to emphasize about this claim is that these developments cannot mean that modernism has somehow become irrelevant or unimportant. The methodological atheism carried within modernism dominates not only the contemporary psychology of religion but also the institutional arrangements of the West. Critics, however, can now articulate a narrative that explains why the rationalism of Descartes' fourth methodological step documents the logical insufficiency of modernism. A brief sketch of three subtexts within that narrative are relevant to the ISM.

With regards to the first subtext, a skepticism directed toward the modernist narrative itself supports a reductionistic analysis of its history that challenges any presumption that its constituent parts can be inductively reassembled into an 'objective' peace. Rather than eliminating violence, modernism made the killings more technologically efficient, as the two World Wars of the 20th Century made clear. In WWII, the nation state where the Treaty of Westphalia had been signed also brought reason to bear on the mass production of death for an entire community that had included Freud himself

(Appleyard 1992). This nation state also used modernist technologies to bomb the city where Freud had been forced to flee. The violence was not one-sided. Those fighting this nation state similarly used modernist technologies to mass produce the deaths of persons ranging in age from infants to grandparents in places like Dresden, Hiroshima, and Nagasaki. And beyond these major wars were innumerable 'minor' conflicts and atheistic and other ideological purges that resulted in a technologically efficient carnage that in absolute numbers dwarfed premodern violence (Hart 2009).

Ultimately, the 'peace' of modernism turned out to include unending violence only constrained at its limits by the mutually assured destruction (MAD) of nuclear weapons (Dupuy 2015). For some, the acronym MAD will capture the insanity of modernist peace (Girard 2010; Boenig-Liptsin 2015; Dumouchel 2015). Perhaps unsurprising, therefore, is the possibility for interpretative frameworks to reverse the modernist narration of its origins at the end of the Thirty Years' War. It was not the case that religious violence was the cause and the creation of nation states was the effect that solved this problem. Rather, the vagaries of political power served as a cause that used religious violence as a means to give birth to nation states as an effect (Cavanaugh 2009). Nation states then necessarily carried violence within their DNA.

In a second subtext, skepticism can also be directed toward the modernist reliance upon reductionism. Cartesian reductionism represents a confidence that the whole is equal to the sum of its parts, and this reductionism has without question made invaluable contributions. Modernist medicine, for example, represents a quantum advancement over premodern medicine. At the same time, however, reductionism may not be sufficient for solving all human problems. Ecological crises, for instance, do not seem easily resolved by reducing them into constituent parts for examination by modernist environmental science, economics, and politics. A broader, and for some a religious vision, will be essential for addressing such problems more holistically (e.g., Girard 2010; Gifford 2015; Northcott 2015).

Indeed, a competing narrative developed within modernism itself to claim that the whole is greater than the sum of its parts. This emergencism argued that novel properties emerge at higher levels of organization and cannot be fully explained through an inductive reconstruction of constituent parts (e.g., Popper and Eccles 1983). Methodological theism, therefore, might embrace this counter-narrative to describe God as an emergent that creates everything else and that God, therefore, cannot be explained away through the reductionism of modernist psychology.

In the third subtext, modernism had to cope with the postmodern skepticism of Nietzsche (1887/1967). Implicit in Nietzsche's philosophy was an awareness that a logically unassailable modernist 'objectivity' requires rational justification of all assumptions including, for example, the final modernist presumption that nature can supply an explanatory framework for everything (Kaufmann 1974). Such a justification would presumably require logical appeal to some other standard, but then nature would become non-ultimate. Perhaps that next higher standard could be the human desire for what science can give us as when Freud (1927/1961a) says, "But an illusion it would be to suppose that what science cannot give us we can get elsewhere" (p. 56). Even if that standard could be made logical, human desire would then itself become the next ultimate standard requiring further rational justification in an infinite regress of justifications that could never find an end. Within this perspective, modernism turns out to be a subjectivity that can have no access to foundations for a logically sufficient final objectivity.

Within modernist and theist conceptual frameworks, postmodernism suggests a disorienting relativism, but that was not necessarily Nietzsche's (1887/1967) obvious intent. His arguments seemed to identify an ultimate standard in the will to power which he defined as the 'instinct for freedom' (Nietzsche, p. 87). Power as an ultimate standard would presumably work against relativism. Freud's desire did, therefore, have potential as an ultimate standard, but for Nietzsche, this was the specific desire for power. Power manifests itself in the instinctual satisfactions of an *Übermensch* and requires no justification beyond its own assertions. Nietzsche dismissed theist and modernist social rationalities as originating in the sniveling moralities of ascetic slaves in defensive reaction to the violence of masters who instinctually pursued their freedom. Nietzsche believed that slave moralities worked in resentful opposition to the creative potentials of power as made obvious, for example, by ancient Rome and Napoleon.

2.3   *Social Rationality, Ideology, and Incommensurability*

Perhaps most consequential in this history of social rationalities is the infinite regress problem implied in Nietzsche's thought. Any belief that nature or any other standard can make ultimate sense now seems to reflect the willingness of a subjectivity to stop justifying itself with anything other than itself. God justifies God. Nature justifies Nature. Power justifies Power. Again, this problem in no way supports a logical dismissal of modernism, nor, for that matter, theism or postmodernism. Instead, the infinite regress problem means that no indubitable, noncontroversial master rationality can be identified for organizing social life.

Relationships among social rationalities seem unalterably changed. Three influential social rationalities now operate with assumptions that can become increasingly 'logical' as they are brought into conformity with visions of their emergent ultimate standard. Those assumptions are inferences derived from interpretations of an ultimate standard and then applied to social life. All three rationalities, therefore, have two capacities for progress. From 'above,' progress can occur as the application of derivative inferences brings the thought and practice of social life into greater conformity with the perceived demands of the ultimate standard. From 'below,' progress can occur as experience with the application of derivative inferences reveals a need for improvements in visions of the ultimate standard and/or in the development of better derivative inferences. Such potentials mean that no social rationality can claim that it alone can be dynamic. A further implication is that social rationalities as a whole can receive no easy dismissal as obviously reactionary or irrational.

Social rationalities in pluralistic societies, therefore, turn out to be ideological. Ideology here reflects three features of the definition proposed by MacIntyre (1978). An ideology first "attempts to delineate certain general characteristics of nature or society, or both, characteristics which do not belong only to particular characteristics of the changing world which can be investigated only by empirical enquiry" (MacIntyre, p. 5). Relative to the ISM, this means that ideologies emerge out of ultimate standards that do not and indeed cannot justify themselves in terms of anything rationally higher or anything empirically lower. These ultimate standards, nevertheless, have implications for empirical and other forms of inquiry as derivative inferences work toward the fulfillment of a social rationality and against its disintegration.

Secondly, "an ideology is an account of the relationship between what is the case and how we ought to act, between the nature of the world and that of morals, politics, and other guides of conduct" (MacIntyre 1978, p. 6). In other words, an ideology makes normative demands in that "it does not merely tell us how the world is *and* how we are to act, but is concerned with the bearing of one upon the other" (p. 6, his emphasis). The ISM argues, for instance, that contemporary social scientific rationalities normatively demand methodological theism, atheism, or postmodernism with the further imperative that observations based upon those methodologies feedback appropriately into interpretations of the ultimate standards of God, Nature, and Power, respectively.

Finally, an ideology will necessarily have a sociological dimension because "it is not merely believed by the members of a given social group, but believed in such a way that it at least partially defines for them their social existence" (MacIntyre 1978, p. 6). As an example, MacIntyre notes, "There is a Christian account of why Christians are Christians and the heathens are not" (p. 6). Similarly, there will be a modernist account of why modernists are modernists and why theist and postmodern heathens are not. Postmodernists will make their own parallel judgments about "heathens."

Intra-ideological heathens may exist as well. Nominally committed to the same ultimate standard, an intra-ideological heathen might be accused of seeing the ultimate standard incorrectly, of deriving illogical inferences from the standard, of adopting unacceptable methods for applying derivative inferences, and/or of misinterpreting how applications of derivative inferences should feedback into interpretations of the ultimate standard. Reformation conflicts between Protestants and Catholics seem appropriately described as intra-ideological battles over who should be defined as the Christian heathen. Arguments between anti-psychological theists and religious psychologists might be described in the same way. Such conflicts are not limited to theism. Within modern psychology, arguments between psychoanalysts, humanists, radical behaviorists, cognitivists, and innumerable other perspectives essentially represent disagreements over who is the intra-ideological modernist psychological heathen.

Pluralistic social life, therefore, finds itself confronted with three rival visions of social rationality (MacIntyre 1990), and these rationalities necessarily operate within ideological surrounds that are incommensurable (MacIntyre 1988). Incommensurability refers to the fact that disagreements between social rationalities will have no access to a shared standard that can supply a noncontroversial metric for defining one ultimate standard as rational and another as irrational. With regard to the relationship between psychology and religion, for example, Nature as the ultimate standard and God as the ultimate standard cannot be submitted to the metric of a higher standard without making them non-ultimate. Nature as an ultimate standard will identify 'God' as a derivative inference to be explained away by methodological atheism. God as the ultimate standard will identify nature as a part of creation to be explained by methodological theism.

Non-reflective presumptions of commensurability between psychology and religion would result in a submission of 'God' to Nature or of nature to God. More specifically, methodological atheism would presume that the language of 'God' could be wholly translated into the language of Nature whereas the methodologies of religious synthesis would operate with an at least implicit belief that the language of nature could be fully contained within the language of God. Both would also be confident in the full translatability of postmodern power into their home ideological languages, and methodological postmodernism would of course seek to translate all other social rationalities into the idioms of Power. In each of these nonreflective approaches, a social rationality would develop the monologue of an ultimate standard that sought to colonize all other so-called ultimate standards (Habermas 1984).

2.4 *Future Objectivity and Post-postmodernism*

Postmodernism may seem to threaten social life with the relativism of Power, but Nietzsche seemed to embrace Power as an absolute. Incommensurability may instead present the greater challenge. Indeed, Nietzsche (1887/1967) sought to rescue 'objectivity' through what he called future objectivity. Modernist objectivity was for him "the dangerous old conceptual fiction that posited a 'pure, will-less, painless, timeless knowing subject'; ... these always demand that we should think of an eye that is completely unthinkable, an eye turned in no particular direction, in which the active interpreting forces, through which alone seeing becomes seeing *something*, are supposed to be lacking." A "conceptual fiction" like modernist skeptical purity fails to acknowledge, "There is only a perspective seeing, only a perspective 'knowing'; and the *more* affects we allow to speak about one thing, the *more* eyes, different eyes, we can use to observe one thing, the more complete will our 'concept' of this thing, our 'objectivity,' be." In place of the monological objectivity of a single affect, Nietzsche recommends the dialogical perspectivism of a future objectivity, involving "the ability to *control* one's Pro and Con and to dispose of them, so that one knows how to employ a *variety* of perspectives and affective interpretations in the service of knowledge" (Nietzsche, p. 119, his emphases).

In broad terms, the ISM seeks to more deeply develop Nietzsche's future objectivity in order to construct a post-postmodern relationship between psychology and religion. One foundational assumption is that Nietzsche's dialogical perspectivism cannot and indeed should not eliminate monological objectivity. A community with a shared ultimate standard will need space to work out the internal logic of its own social rationality without necessarily considering refinements suggested by dialogues with other social rationalities. Refinements presuppose the existence of something to refine in the first place. Monological objectivity is, thus, a logical prerequisite of dialogical objectivity. Still, monological objectivity can have very different implications within a Triumphalist Model and within a Dialogical Model of the relationship between psychology and religion.

Figure 1 depicts the Triumphalist Model. Triumphalist communities could have God, Nature, or Power as their ultimate standard. Each community would use methodologies acceptable within the ideological surround of its ultimate standard to express and then apply derivative inferences to social life. Consequences of those applications could then feedback into the triumphalist perspective to perhaps influence visions of the ultimate standard or

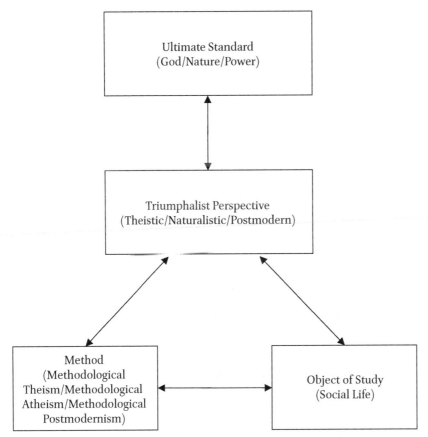

FIGURE 1   Triumphalist Model with monological objectivity defined within theistic, naturalistic, and postmodern ideological surrounds

to perhaps improve the articulation and application of derivative inferences in the methods of triumphalist inquiry. A methodological atheist might use well-established psychological scales to test hypotheses about relationships of cognitive complexity with religious orientation measures that assess how psychologists often interpret religious motivations (Gorsuch and McPherson 1989). An anti-psychological theist might use biblical exegesis to reject notions of personal flourishing expressed within humanistic psychology. Each research program would fall within the Triumphalist Model.

Triumphalism would also exhibit tendencies toward ghettoization and colonization. Ghettoization ideologically walls out any meaningful insights into how other social rationalities might understand and explain themselves and social life. Colonization then occurs as a triumphalist social rationality pursues the full translation of an outside social rationality into its own idiom as if other

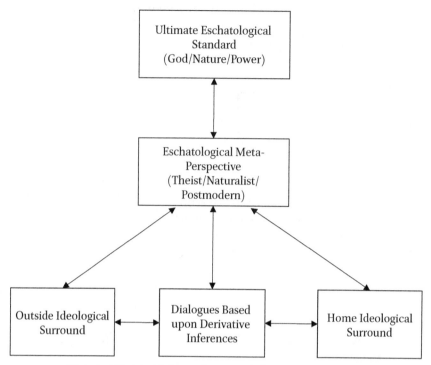

FIGURE 2 Dialogical Model with future objectivity defined by an eschatological meta-perspective coordinated between a higher eschatological ultimate standard above and dialogical considerations of home and outside social rationalities below

ideological surrounds have nothing unique or important to say. Ghettoization and colonization would then interfere with the maturation of a triumphalist social rationality that would become increasingly out of touch with complex empirical realities.

Most importantly, however, the ISM draws out potentials in Nietzsche's future objectivity to develop the post-postmodern Dialogical Model presented in Figure 2. No social rationality in a pluralistic world can define the *future* in future objectivity as something already achieved. Any claim to have eyes that already see final ideological triumph can only occur through the ghettoization of a social rationality and its colonization of other ideological surrounds. As defined by the ISM, future instead refers to the always ongoing process of dialogue with other social rationalities in an attempt to become increasingly insightful about the home social rationality, its cultural context, and its eventual fulfillment. Hence, the future objectivity of post-postmodernism turns out to be an eschatological objectivity.

As Figure 2 makes clear, eschatological meta-perspectivism finds its coordination in two opposite directions. From above, the dialogical meta-perspective will remain faithful to the ultimate eschatological triumph as understood within the home ideological surround. The ISM emerges as an exercise in metaphysical theist eschatology, but Figure 2 also leaves options open for modernist and postmodernist eschatologies. The possibility of a modernist eschatology seems obvious enough in Freud's (1927/1961) claim about the intellect that Nature makes available to humanity: "The primacy of the intellect lies, it is true, in a distant, distant future, but probably not in an *infinitely* distant one" (p. 53, his emphasis; for a different modernist eschatology, see Fukuyama 2006). The possibility of a postmodern eschatology seems more tenuous. The French theorist Jacques Derrida was an intellectual descendent of Nietzsche. At a famous Johns Hopkins University conference in 1966, a respondent to a paper delivered by Derrida essentially asked what his and thus what the postmodern eschatology might be. Derrida responded, "I was wondering myself if I know where I am going. So I would answer you by saying, first, that I am trying, precisely, to put myself at a point so that I do not know any longer where I am going" (Derrida as quoted by Haven 2018, p. 137). Aimlessness apparently is the postmodern eschatological aim.

From below, eschatological meta-perspectivism will be coordinated with complexities associated with three dialogical interactions. The most important of these interactions will be with the home ideological surround. The language of eschatological meta-perspectivism will need to be fully translatable within the current home language. This requirement may seem to make progress impossible. After all, how can the *same* change the *same*? Triumphalist theists may be especially worried about this problem; but in processes of the same changing the same, the home ultimate standard will always be the nonnegotiable determinant of its own eschatological maturation. Use of that ultimate standard in dialogues with other social rationalities may reveal that visions of that ultimate standard require refinement or that home derivative inferences are currently incorrect. Dialogues may also uncover new compatible or at least not incompatible derivative inferences that can be assimilated within an expanding home objectivity. Derivative inferences within a home rationality will also be organized in a hierarchy in which higher inferences can serve as stipulations for the application of lower inferences. Dialogues with other social rationalities can reveal a need to reorganize that hierarchy. In each of these circumstances, the same would control changes in the same.

Second, from below as well, an eschatological meta-perspective will be coordinated within its understanding of an outside social rationality. That coordination will include a need to see how an outside social rationality sees the home social rationality and vice versa. Movements back and forth between these two acts of seeing will identify possible terms for their rational dialogue. Nietzsche (1887/1967), for example, saw within history "Christian conscience translated and sublimated into scientific conscience," with both forms of conscience reflecting a commitment to the will to truth (pp. 160–161). Even atheism turns out to be a sublimated expression of the theist will to truth when it asserts that 'God' is not the 'truth.' Theism and modernism, therefore, share 'truth' as a derivative inference so high in their hierarchical structures that 'truth' should be nonnegotiable term of dialogue. This derivative inference also obligates methodological theism and atheism to pursue truthful understandings of how they see both their home and outside social rationalities. Modernist commitments to truth will also mean that the reliability and validity of social scientific methods can be assimilated within methodological theism and used in dialogues to more truthfully advance the 'truth' of both theism and modernism.

Third and finally, eschatological meta-perspectivism will need to be oriented below toward the social scientifically constructed dialogical space between social rationalities. Again, this space could not use the ultimate standard of any particular social rationality as the dialogical standard. Incommensurability will mean that this ultimate standard could only operate as a term of conflict made endless because of the infinite regress problem. Dialogical space should instead be organized as a hierarchy of shared derivative inferences that would serve as a provisional rationality for constructing a more, though not absolutely neutral dialogical space.

Outcomes of these social scientific dialogues would activate feedback loops in multiple directions. Results of dialogues would inform eschatological meta-perspectival evaluations of the methods themselves and could suggest useful refinements and innovations in future procedures. Findings could also improve meta-perspectival understandings of the outside social rationality and suggest additional derivative inferences for later evaluation. Finally, dialogical data would identify outside derivative inferences as compatible, incompatible, or neutral relative to the home monologue. The home rationality could then assimilate those judgments within an increasingly expansive and more logically sufficient home monologue. Tendencies toward ghettoization and colonization would be reduced. Tendencies toward maturation would be enhanced.

The metaphysical theism of the ISM pursues the Dialogical Model in at least two ways. As Section 3 will make clear, metaphysical theists can be in dialogue with contemporary psychology by using standard psychometric procedures to operationalize derivative inferences that theoretically move psychological functioning of a religious community toward its eschatological ideals. Those operationalizations can then be brought into empirical dialogue with well-established psychological measures of mental health and religious commitment. Correlations among those constructs has a potential to supply information that promotes the maturation of both theist and modernist ideological surrounds. Section 4 will then review the procedures of a theist methodological dialogism that even more directly bring methodological theist and methodological atheist social rationalities in direct conversation.

2.5 *Post-postmodern Dialogue and Triumphalisms*
Eschatological objectivity would presumably grow as advances in methodological theism served as a stimulus for advances in methodological atheism and vice versa. This dialogical progress would rest on 'truth' as a shared derivative inference, and 'truth' for both social rationalities would also be a nonnegotiable derivative inference in dialogues with postmodernism. Truth as a term of dialogue with Nietzschean postmodernism, nevertheless, confronts noteworthy challenges.

In place of religion and science, Nietzsche (1887/1967) advocated an embrace of art, "in which the lie is sanctified and the will to deception has a good conscience" (p. 153). His openness to the "will to deception" perhaps makes it unsurprising that "the term post-modern is employed so broadly that it seems to apply to everything and nothing all at once" (Rosenau 1992, p. 17). Relative to the ISM, a useful perspective appears in the suggestion that postmodernism, "if it means anything ... concerns aspects of *aesthetic reflection* upon the nature of modernity" (Giddens 1990, p. 45, his emphasis). The nature of modernity includes relationships among incommensurable theist, modernist, and postmodern social rationalities. For theists and modernists, however, aesthetic reflection as a will to deception will have no intuitively obvious potentials for supplying terms of dialogue with the will to truth.

Indeed, in Nietzsche's (1887/1967) view, the will to truth merely developed as an ascetic impoverishment of psychological and social life used by resentful slaves wielding Power to defend themselves against the free assertion of instincts by masters. Nietzsche believed that this slavish will to truth would necessarily reach its final 'truthful' conclusion that the will to truth is actually a lie and just another manifestation of the will to power. This final 'truth' would be its "*most striking inference*, its inference *against* itself." The result of life without truth would be that "morality will gradually perish now: this is the great spectacle in a hundred acts reserved for the next two centuries in Europe—the most terrible, most questionable, and perhaps also the most hopeful of all spectacles" (Nietzsche, p. 161, his emphases). Whether this spectacle has been terrible or hopeful will depend on the social rationality making the assessment.

Again, Figure 2 includes Power as a potential ultimate standard for a post-postmodern Nietzschean meta-perspectivism. But again, how can the will to lie supply derivative inferences for conducting meaningful dialogues with a will to truth? The aesthetic 'logic' of that process would have to be worked out within a Nietzschean post-postmodern ideological surround, if that is even possible.

In the absence of that logic, Nietzschean future objectivity as opposed to a broader post-postmodern ISM future objectivity might be interpreted as the triumphalist methodological postmodernism of Power depicted in Figure 1. Here, the Nietzschean suspension of pros and cons would be under the sole control of Power in interaction with outside social rationalities given no real opportunity to speak for themselves. Similarly, in his analysis of religion as an illusion, Freud (1927/1961a) imagined interactions with religious interlocutors, and he put questions into their mouths that he was well able to answer. This too seemed to be a triumphalist future objectivity, but this time under the sole control of an intellect directed toward Nature. Anti-psychological theists who reject contemporary psychology (Powlison 2010) also seem to develop a triumphalist future objectivity dedicated to God that is deaf to other social rationalities. In all of these instances, triumphalist objectivities would have at least some potential to work out the internal logic of their home rationality, but each would also have potentials toward ghettoization, colonization, and consequent dismissal in an increasingly pluralistic world.

Theist and modernist meta-perspectives, nevertheless, might want to conduct dialogues with Nietzschean postmodernism as the outside social rationality; and they would want to do so while remaining committed to 'truth' as a provisional dialogical standard. Nietzschean thought, for example, influenced Maslow's (1971/1993) understanding of humanistic self-actualization (Smith 1973). This postmodern influence, among perhaps many others, deserves eschatological meta-perspectival dialogical clarification. Within the post-postmodernism of slave moralities, dialogues with postmodernism might begin with the realization that the will to deception is either a deception or the truth. If it is the truth, then this deception becomes self-refuting. If this deception is itself a deception, then it hides some affinity with truth. For theists and modernists, therefore, the deceptive 'truth' will be that Power only claims to be an ultimate standard, and 'truth' should be a nonnegotiable provisional standard for conducting dialogues with Nietzschean postmodernism. The need for such dialogues might become more obvious with the realization that Power is not constrained within philosophy but also operates in history, as Nietzsche's admiration of ancient Rome and Napoleon made clear. Slave moralities will, therefore, believe that it is important to hold power as a derivative inference accountable to God or to Nature. In a MAD world, morality should not perish now.

2.6 *Conclusion*

Psychology and religion intersect in a cultural space that illustrates a central challenge within contemporary social life. That challenge involves knowing what to do about incommensurable social rationalities within a pluralistic world. Nietzsche's postmodernism points toward the infinite regress problem and makes it logically clear that no social rationality can claim final objectivity. In psychology, narrations of modernist triumph are an important monological goal, but they will have limited dialogical potential. Secularization, for instance, is a derivative inference that will make sense within some modernist but not within theist ideological surrounds. Theist social rationalities are enormously complex living realities that will not easily disappear in response to the reason and experience of science. After Nietzsche, belief in that disappearance will seem for some to be a wish-fulfilment and thus an illusion.

Both modernist psychological and theist social rationalities reflect what Nietzsche called slave moralities. That common heritage gives them a shared post-postmodern potential to make progress toward a more trans-rationally logical and peaceful future. This could occur through a reliance upon 'truth' as a derivative inference that supplies a provisional standard for conducting dialogues. The ISM has explored that potential from the vantage point of a theist meta-perspectivism. Research programs that formally develop an atheist post-postmodernist meta-perspectivism remain a distinct possibility as well. 'Truth' might also operate as an admittedly more problematic provisional standard for conducting dialogues with postmodernism.

Development of the ISM has occurred as an experiment in methodological theism. A careful examination of ISM data will reveal that theist meta-perspectivism has a potential to enhance modernist as well as theist social rationalities. These data will also make it clear that the ISM is not an exercise in apologetics because findings can document needs for theism to refine its own internal logic. The same presumably could occur with a post-postmodern atheist meta-perspectivism that more forthrightly acknowledged Nature as an incommensurable rather than a universally indisputable ultimate standard. The suggestion, in other words, is that a nonreflective dismissal of dialogism by any ideological surround would be irrational relative to what the evidence already identifies as a methodology for constructing a more trans-rationally mature future objectivity.

The ISM does not naively assume that anti-dialogism can be eliminated. Within Christian social rationalities, for instance, 1 Peter 2:18 says, "Slaves accept the authority of your masters with all deference, not only those who are kind and gentle but also those who are harsh." Meanings of that verse within Christian monological rationalities dominant in Richmond, Virginia, when it was capital of the slave-holding Confederacy, were very different from its meanings in Richmond today as an American state capital that is much less distant sociologically from Washington, DC. The Christian ultimate standard currently makes no compromises with slavery as a derivative inference, which has fallen far down in the hierarchy of its social rationality. Slavery now is brought under the control of numerous higher derivative inferences that constrain what it can imply in contemporary argumentation. Those changes in hierarchy reflect, in part, the consequences of dialogues among Christians (Woolman 1774/1961) and of modernist rationalities that worked out the logic of democratic rights as derivative inferences. Most importantly, however, those changes occurred through the end of slavery produced by the anti-dialogue of the American Civil War from 1861 to 1865.

Among other things, this and other aspects of history demonstrate that social rationalities are complex cultural constructions that resist their own disintegration. Between the "now" and "not-yet" of any eschatology, a social rationality will work through innumerable, often unexpected challenges as it pursues the long route toward its ideological satisfaction. The "not-yet" of an eschatology is not a wish-fulfillment. It is not an illusion. It is instead a wish that will be eschatologically 'rational' within a home ideological surround as it tries to live out its history.

Finally, methodological dialogisms create a shared cultural space where incommensurable social rationalities can more insightfully respond to their compatible, incompatible, and orthogonal derivative inferences. This process could promote the never-ending construction of social capital useful in avoiding anti-dialogues. The dialogical 'not-yet' of slave moralities might, for example, justify themselves in a dream once described in a speech of Martin Luther King, Jr. (1963), delivered on the steps of the Lincoln Memorial in Washington, DC. That dream made its wish clear in "the words of the old Negro spiritual, 'Free at last, Free at last, Great God a-mighty, we are free at last.'" Here, faith pursues a long route toward a 'truthful' rather than an illusory or anti-dialogical satisfaction of the instinct for freedom.

3 Empiricism, Dialogue, and the Operationalization of Religious Traditions

As interpreted by the ISM, religion and psychology are both somewhat non-empirical, normative, sociological, and thus ideological (MacIntyre 1978). God is the ultimate standard of traditional religious rationalities, and inferences derived from that ultimate standard will explain how nature is the creation of God. Nature is the ultimate standard of social scientific rationalities, and inferences derived from that ultimate standard will explain how 'God' is the product of Nature. Each social rationality will include norms that define acceptable practices of observation and interpretation; so, no uninterpreted raw data will be available for 'neutrally' discovering which standard should be ultimate. This absence of a neutral metric of evaluation makes these ideologies incommensurable (MacIntyre 1988). Incommensurability then guarantees the separation of psychology and religion into sociologically distinct communities. Within each community, ultimate standards and derivative inferences will operate as a dialectic that moves a social rationality toward expansive maturation or toward a constricting ghettoization that seeks the colonization of other social rationalities. The somewhat non-empirical, normative, and sociological dimensions of each ideology will mean that commitments to both will be at least somewhat 'subjective.' To even implicitly assume otherwise would not be 'objective.'

The ISM pursues conceptual and methodological innovations that attempt to rescue the 'objectivity' of interactions between psychology and religion from the problem of incommensurability. Monological research programs will attempt to explain away outside social rationalities by translating them fully into the language of their home rationality. Dialogical research programs will pursue greater 'truthfulness' by bringing social rationalities into interactions that respect their incommensurability. The inclusion of both types of research programs within the ISM is necessary, because as empirical realities, 'objectivity' requires it.

Monological, triumphalist options leave room for methodological atheism to dismiss the rationality of methodological theism and vice versa. In a post-postmodern world, no noncontroversial master rationality will be available for arguing against either monologue as unquestionably irrational. Nor, can a master rationality demonstrate that dialogism and its sensitivity to pluralism is indubitably more rational. Nothing prevents a monologist from complaining that dialogism operates as an increasingly powerful ghettoizing force within contemporary intellectual life that encourages a pluralistic colonization of all other social rationalities. Dialogists will of course offer their own counterarguments. Conflicts like this have a potential to be interminable and unproductive.

3.1 ISM *and Empiricism as Ideological*

Dialogical research programs account for the eschatological aspirations of both the social sciences and traditional religions. Dialogists will realize that the full rationalities of both have yet to be achieved. As dynamic living processes, social rationalities and their current limitations should not be hypostatized within an ideological space that makes them easier to dismiss. Rather than dismissal, dialogical research seeks better understanding within and between ideologies through empirically guided interactions. Those interactions will occur under the faithful ideological guidance of derivative inferences associated with the eschatological aspirations of either a theist or an atheist ultimate standard. The challenges of incommensurability make the dialogical construction of a peaceful public space essential for pluralistic social life. The ISM attempts to contribute to that peaceful public space by developing and defending the dialogism of a methodological theism.

ISM methodologies analyze the 'truth' of incommensurable rationalities by taking advantage of social scientific standards of reliability and validity. Those standards in empirical research can help adjudicate the dialogical 'truth' of derivative inferences associated with incommensurable social rationalities. Such adjudications have a post-postmodern potential to socially construct a trans-rational 'objectivity' that is not based upon one or another specific ultimate standard. Adjudications based upon ultimate standards would have little productive potential given the absence of a master social rationality that can definitively end arguments between social rationalities. The empiricism of trans-rational adjudications based upon derivative inferences could instead describe a common ground for strengthening centripetal processes of cohesion within pluralistic cultures. Trans-rational objectivity may also help ameliorate centrifugal tendencies toward fragmentation by promoting a wider tolerance for what the evidence reveals to be a meaningfulness across social rationalities. Centrifugal forces might also be ameliorated through the empirical identification of specific shared derivative inferences that can mediate the disagreements that invariably exist across social rationalities within pluralistic social life.

The ISM commitment to empiricism will itself be ideological and will reflect at least six assumptions. First, the empiricism of methodological theism can and must supplement the empiricism of methodological atheism. Absolutely no research investigation will have access to any ultimate standard taken as a whole. Research must instead examine how inferences derived from visions of an ultimate standard point toward normative regularities in the thought and practice of social life. This is as true of visions of Nature as of visions of God. An evolutionary psychologist, for instance, may derive inferences about survival of the fittest gene in Nature to conclude that the rationality of male more than female sexuality encourages promiscuity in the short-term (Buss and Schmitt 1993). In tests of this hypothesis, males and females will serve as informants about how the norms of Nature operate within their sexuality. Conversely, a religious psychologist may derive inferences from a vision of God to describe the rationality of always committed sexual relationships for both males and females. Religious believers will then serve as informants about how the norms of God operate within their sexuality. Both research programs will pursue an intra-ideological objectivity.

Second, empirical methods can usefully address the previously mentioned problem that conflicts between incommensurable social rationalities can be interminable and unproductive. Again, monological rationalities might describe pluralism as ghettoizing and colonizing just as dialogical rationalities might describe monological rationalities in the same terms. The absence of a master rationality will mean that the arguments of each will have limited if any impact on the other. On the other hand, social scientific evidence can present reliable and valid demonstrations of problematic implications within the derivative inferences of both monological and dialogical rationalities. Such evidence can be ignored only at the expense of 'objectivity' and still will not falsify any ultimate standard given the problem of incommensurability. Quantitative and qualitative data, therefore, could result in conflicts between ideological surrounds that remained interminable, but that could also become more productive because derivative inferences can be falsified whereas ultimate standards cannot. Interminable productivity would be a clear advance over interminable unproductivity.

Third, empirical methods can help serve as a safeguard against authoritarianism. The ISM suggests that social rationalities committed to Nature and not just to God can speak *ex cathedra*. Such pronouncements may have their place within triumphalist monologues. However, empirical methods even within triumphalist research programs can supply evidence that tends to move pronouncements based upon Nature or God toward authoritativeness. In other words, empirical demonstrations of the rationality of a pronouncement will confirm its validity whereas disconfirmations will challenge its plausibility. In response to such disconfirmations, a refusal to make necessary adjustments within a social rationality would move it toward authoritarianism. As interpreted by the ISM, authoritarianism represents the colonizing immaturity of ghettoization and should be rejected. Such arguments presume that 'truth' rests, at least in part, upon a correspondence between pronouncements and empirical observations.

Fourth, the ISM commitment to empiricism means that the incommensurability of social rationalities reveals a need to expand basic conceptualizations of psychological research. Nomothetic research programs formulate generalizations that apply to populations as a whole whereas ideographic approaches focus on efforts to understand the individual. The ISM suggests that between populations and individuals are sociologically distinct communities with social rationalities that deserve analysis in their own right. Ideologographic research programs, therefore, need to be positioned between the better known nomothetic and ideographic options (Watson, Chen, Ghorbani, and Vartanian 2015). Addition of this ideologographic option would result in a more defensible 'objectivity' within contemporary psychology.

Fifth, ideologographic research will need to pursue at least two empirical strategies. First, and most obviously, use of standard psychometric procedures should offer at least tentative operationalizations of derivative inferences that operate within a communal social rationality. Analysis of those derivative inferences will document meaningful regularities in the thought and practice of a community that might be ignored by other research perspectives (e.g., Watson, Morris, and Hood 1988a, 1988b). In addition, methodological innovations should work to psychometrically deconstruct already existent research measures in order to uncover previously obscured influences of ideology. Research already demonstrates that these deconstructive procedures can identify where schisms exist between a community and the population (Watson, Morris, and Hood 1989) or sometimes even within what may appear to be a single community (Watson et al. 2003). Such methods can also document ideological compatibilities between a community and the population (Andrews et al. 2017) and falsify communal presumptions of an incompatibility between religious and social scientific rationalities (Watson et al. 1995). All such outcomes would work toward the empirical construction of an increasingly complex trans-rational 'objectivity.'

Sixth and finally, the ISM appeal to standard psychometric procedures and their deconstruction is not an appeal to technical, social scientific perspectives as definitive in theory. The more important point is that psychometrics merely defines a dialogical space in which assertions across social rationalities can be discussed with the rules of adjudication already established. The ISM commitment to empiricism, therefore, does not represent a presumption that ideological conflicts can be resolved through the essentially reductionistic social scientific methods. Instead, those methods are principally important because they can supply a taken-for-granted, background language for moving productively toward more meaningful dialogues between the emergent perspectives of different ideological surrounds.

3.2 *Operationalizing Traditions and Dialogue*

Perhaps most basically, the ISM attempts to give a voice to theist ideological surrounds through the formal operationalization of derivative inferences associated with religious traditions. Dialogical concerns sometimes serve as the initiating stimulus for assessing some aspect of a theist social rationality. Other times, a research program will begin as a relatively straightforward attempt to better understand a religious tradition, but subsequent interpretations will point toward important dialogical implications. Three lines of research involving two different religious traditions will illustrate these dialogical potentials.

3.3 Sin and Grace within a Christian Ideological Surround

Psychological perspectives can describe guilt and its supposed manifestation in a sense of sin as problematic. This literature is complex (Watson, Hood, and Morris 1988a, 1988b), but Freud (1930/1961b) illustrates a negative evaluation of sin when he describes "instinctual renunciation" as essential to the development of civilization but also as the frequent product of guilt feelings associated with a superego that "torments the *sinful* ego with ... anxiety and is on the watch for opportunities of getting it punished by the external world" (p. 81, emphasis added). Freud then sought "to represent the sense of guilt as the most important problem in the development of civilization and to show that the price we pay for our advance in civilization is a loss of happiness through the heightening of the sense of guilt" (p. 91). To maximize happiness, Freud argued, the realistic and rational controls of the ego should replace the guilt of the superego in addressing the instinctual demands of the id: "Where id was, there ego [and not superego] should be" (Freud 1933/1964). At least some psychological perspectives, therefore, have moved along a trajectory of thought toward the conclusion that the "concept of sin is the direct and indirect cause of virtually all neurotic disturbance" (Ellis 1962, p. 146).

Christian interpretations of sin can be diverse and controversial (e.g., Biddle 2005; Ramm 1985). Christians, nevertheless, can describe the experience of sin in terms very different from neurotic guilt as "a love-motivated emotion closely related to guilt feelings yet radically different. Whereas psychological guilt is a self-punitive process, constructive sorrow is a love-motivated desire to change that is rooted in concern for others" (Narramore 1984, p. 33). Moreover, the word 'sin' originates, not in an emotional experience of guilt, but rather in an awareness of having missed the mark (Biddle 2005). To sin in thought and behavior is to miss the mark in the same way that an arrow shot from a bow misses the mark of its target. That mark for some Christians will be the perfection of God:

> "This powerful sense of having sinned against the perfection of God ... distinguishes repentance from remorse" (cf. 2 Cor. 7:8–10). The Greek word for repentance means to have a second opinion about something. Our first opinion is our own and it is an approving opinion. When confronted with the perfection of God we form a second opinion about sin,

which is God's opinion. Remorse is the sorrow resulting from the problems, alienations, and hurts that come to us in our own sinful lives, but is barren of reference to God.

RAMM 1985, p. 95

Christian traditions further assume that all fail to reach the perfection of God. Romans 3:23 emphasizes, for example, that "all have sinned and fall short of the glory of God," and 1 John 1:8 adds, "If we claim to be without sin, we deceive ourselves and the truth is not in us." This realization should not result in a ruminative remorse or neurotic guilt motivated by a punitive 'God' internalized within the superego. Sin instead should lead to a constructive sorrow framed within an awareness of God's freely available forgiveness. Ephesians 2:8–10 asserts, for instance, "For it is by grace you have been saved, through faith—and this is not from yourselves, it is the gift of God—not by works, so that no one can boast. For we are God's handiwork, created in Christ Jesus to do good works, which God prepared in advance for us to do." Constructive sorrow would presumably be among the potentials for good works prepared in advance for us by God, and faith in the grace of God should remove fear and encourage a repentance that moves thought and behavior closer to the mark of Christian adjustment as made manifest in love-motivated individuals and communities.

Hence, Christian understandings of sin point toward very different hypotheses than would at least some psychological interpretations. Operationalizations of Christian beliefs in sin and grace should, and in fact do, predict adjustment (e.g., Watson, Morris, and Hood 1988a, 1988b, 1989). Sin and grace scales, for example, can correlate negatively with depression. Included in these sin-related beliefs are such self-reports as "Nobody in the world is really good, least of all, am I." The idea that a scale that includes an item like this can correlate negatively rather than positively with depression clearly goes against prominent perspectives within contemporary psychology. Beliefs in grace appear in such claims as "My sins are forgiven." Partial correlations controlling for grace eliminate linkages of sin with lower depression, and this result supports Christian presuppositions that the adjustment benefits of beliefs in sin occur through faith in God's grace. Positive correlations with adaptive forms of self-consciousness also conform, in very general terms, with the idea that beliefs in sin and grace can support a beneficially repentant self-awareness about thoughts and actions that might miss the mark.

Additional assessments have more deeply clarified sin-related beliefs. A Beliefs about Sin Scale (Watson et al. 2007) identified four factors that recorded Self-Improvement (e.g., "My beliefs about sin have helped me work on my weaknesses"), Perfectionism Avoidance (e.g., "Knowledge of my personal sinfulness has lifted the burden from my shoulders of trying to be perfect"), Healthy Humility (e.g., "My awareness of sin helps me maintain an appropriate humility"), and Self-Reflective Functioning (e.g., "My beliefs about sin have made it possible for me to be more objective about myself"). All four factors predicted better mental health as made obvious in correlations that were positive with self-esteem and negative with depression, anxiety, and maladjusted narcissism. Multiple regression procedures examined the incremental validity of these factors by examining their linkages with adjustment after controlling for variance associated with the intrinsic religious orientation as a more general index of religiousness. Self-Improvement proved to be the sole determinant of connections with psychological adjustment; Healthy Humility unexpectedly turned out to be unhealthy. Such data documented how the operationalization of traditions can sometimes discover unsuspected complexities in their dynamics.

Other investigations have also documented the complexity of grace-related beliefs (Bufford, Sisemore, and Blackburn 2017). Included in measures of grace were factors that recorded Experiencing God's Grace (e.g., "Because of God's work in my life I feel I have more self-control. My actions are more likely to be appropriate"), Costly Grace (e.g., such reverse scored items as "The harder I work, the more I earn God's favor"), Grace to Self (e.g., "I seldom feel shame"), Grace from Others (e.g., "As a child I was confident that at least one of my parents loved me no matter what"), and Grace to Others (e.g., "When offended or harmed by others I generally find it easy to forgive them"). The adaptive implications of these factors appeared, for instance, in correlations that were positive with gratitude, well-being, and positive religious coping and negative with internalized shame, negative religious coping, adverse childhood experiences, and global distress.

3.4   *Muslim Experiential Religiousness in Iran*

Cartesian presumptions seem at least implicit in some Western research programs that reduce religion and spirituality into constituent parts for reconstruction into more complex wholes. This appears, for example, in procedures that ask research participants to identify themselves as being both religious and spiritual, religious but not spiritual, spiritual but not religious, or neither religious nor spiritual (Zinnbauer et al. 1997). Here, atoms of religion and spirituality combine into four different compounds. Reductionism also seems to stand behind attempts to operationalize scales that record a generic rather than an explicitly religious spirituality (Hodge 2003). Such instruments rest upon definitions of spirituality generally as a "search for the sacred" (Pargament

2013, p. 257) and more specifically as "beliefs, practices, relationships, or experiences having to do with the sacred that are not necessarily linked to established institutionalized systems" (Loewenthal 2013, p. 239). Such reductionism may be especially germane to life in an increasingly secularized West where a sense of the sacred can combine with a vast array of nonreligious commitments, including art, work, sexuality, nature, nation, and self, to mention only a few possibilities.

At the same time, however, religion and spirituality typically function as interdependent unities, even in the West (Marler and Hadaway 2002). The ISM, therefore, assumes that atomistic and wholistic perspectives on religion and spirituality will have validity within their own ideological surrounds and should be brought into dialogue. Pursuit of that goal obviously requires the operationalization of specifically religious rather than just generic expressions of spirituality. Construction of a Muslim Experiential Religiousness (MER) Scale has illustrated that possibility in Iran (Ghorbani, Watson, Geranmayepour and Chen 2013, 2014a, 2014b).

Analysis of this issue in Iran was especially useful for at least two reasons. First, religiousness in the West can display perturbations caused by a defensiveness toward secularism (Watson, Chen, and Morris 2018; Watson, Chen, Morris, and Stephenson 2015). As a formally Islamic society, Iranian religiousness should and in fact appears to be less influenced by disturbances associated with secularization (Watson, Ghorbani, Vartanian, and Chen 2015). Second, analysis of a non-Western Muslim spirituality usefully demonstrates the importance of operationalizing religious traditions beyond Western Christian ideological surrounds.

Central to MER is a realization that 'Islam' in the Arabic of the *Qur'an* means 'surrender' (Nasr 2002) *Qur'an* (4:125) asks, for example, "Whose way is better than that of the man who has submitted to God, and does good, and who follows the creed of Abraham the upright?" The spirituality of a Muslim thus appears in a man like Abraham who surrenders to God, and this is the God who is always "closer to him than his jugular vein" (*Qur'an*, 50:16). This means that "He is with you wheresoever you may be, and He perceives whatsoever you do" (*Qur'an*, 57:4). Among other things, this closeness is psychologically important because it makes the love of God continuously available: "Say: 'If you love God then follow me that God may love you and forgive your faults; for God is forgiving and kind'" (*Qur'an*, 3:31). Symbolic of this tradition-specific spirituality are the daily prayers of Islam in which the prostrate submission of a Muslim attempts to move consciousness closer to the love of God.

In conformity with methodological theism, a 15-item MER Scale responds to this *Qur'anic* perspective by operationalizing religious spirituality as a

Muslim norm of searching for the sacred in a close and loving submission to God. Illustrating submission in this bonding with God is the self-report, "Experiences of submitting to God cause me to feel more vital and motivated." The love of God appears in such claims as, "When I look deeply within myself, I understand that the experience of loving God is worth any effort in my life." The motivation to get closer to God appears, for example, in the assertion, "Intimate closeness to God is at the core of my efforts to be religious." In Iran, MER yielded evidence that an explicitly Muslim spirituality appears to *Incite*, *Integrate*, and *Invigorate* Muslim religiousness. In other words, these data pointed toward the heuristic potentials of a *3-I Model* of Muslim religious spirituality (Ghorbani, Watson, Gharibi, and Chen 2018).

Initiating effects indicate the existence of a reciprocal causality in which greater religious spirituality 'initiates' or promotes greater religiousness and vice versa. The most straightforward evidence for such a conclusion appears in positive MER correlations with a wide range of instruments that record Muslim religious commitments (Ghorbani, Watson, Geranmayepour and Chen 2013, 2014a, 2014b). Those who self-identify as being both religious and spiritual also display the highest MER scores (Ghorbani, Watson, Asadi, and Chen 2018; Ghorbani, Watson, Kashanaki, and Chen 2017; Ghorbani, Watson, Rabiee, and Chen 2018). Moreover, Islamic seminarians score higher on MER than do university students (Ghorbani, Watson, Aghababaei, and Chen 2014; Ghorbani Watson, Kashanaki, and Chen 2017; Ghorbani, Watson, Madani, and Chen 2016) and members of the more general Iranian population (Ghorbani, Watson, Gharibi, and Chen 2018). MER, therefore, points towards a stronger bonding with God that 'initiates' movement toward a religious career.

Integrating effects refer to demonstrations that religious spirituality connects or links religiousness with its adjustment implications. Such effects appear in mediation analyses in which MER fully or partially mediates (Baron and Kenney 1986) relationships of religiousness with array of psychological and other religious constructs. In one Iranian study, for instance, MER mediated linkages of the intrinsic and extrinsic religious orientations with stronger Muslim attitudes and with lower depression and higher satisfaction with life. MER also helped explain religious and psychological differences observed between Islamic seminarians and university students (Ghorbani, Watson, Geranmayepour, and Chen 2014a). Similar mediation outcomes have appeared with numerous other constructs (Ghorbani, Watson, Geranmayepour, and Chen 2013, 2014b).

Invigorating effects refer to a role of religious spirituality in energizing or enlivening religiousness. Such outcomes appear in moderation analyses (Baron and Kenney 1986) in which MER interacts with other religious constructs to magnify their adjustment implications. In Iran, for instance, Muslim attitudes have more strongly predicted religious and psychological adjustment when MER was higher; and when MER was lower, religious measures at least sometimes failed to predict adjustment or instead predicted maladjustment (Ghorbani, Watson, Geranmayepour, and Chen 2014b; Ghorbani et al. 2017; Ghorbani, Watson, Madani, and Chen 2016). The suggestion, in other words, was that the religious spirituality of MER fueled or invigorated the psychological influences of Muslim commitments.

Three other findings suggested that moderation effects may be especially useful in uncovering complexities in Muslim religiousness. First, unlike the largely adjusted intrinsic and extrinsic personal religious orientations in Iran, the extrinsic social orientation displays largely nonsignificant but sometimes weakly positive or negative relationships with psychological adjustment (Ghorbani, Watson, and Khan 2007). The extrinsic social orientation, therefore, seems to be ambiguous and largely irrelevant for Iranian Muslims. Moderation effects, nevertheless, reveal that extrinsic social linkages with *poorer* mental health become clear when the religious spirituality of MER is lower. When MER is higher, the extrinsic social orientation has no adjustment implications at all. Hence, MER may serve as an invigorating protective factor within the psychological dynamics of extrinsic social religiousness (Ghorbani, Watson, Gharibi, and Chen 2018).

Second, a recent Pakistani study confirmed that the validity of the MER is not limited to the specifically Iranian context (Khan, Watson, and Chen 2016). More importantly, however, moderation effects revealed that both Positive and Negative Religious Coping Scales (Pargament, Feuille, and Burdzy 2011) predicted lower levels of distress about the public effects of terrorism when MER was higher. When MER was lower, both predicted higher levels of distress. This finding needs to be replicated and extended before confident conclusions can be offered, but the interesting preliminary suggestion is that a supposedly maladaptive negative religious coping can at least sometimes be adaptive when framed within a Muslim religious spirituality and that a supposedly adaptive positive religious coping can at least sometimes be maladaptive in the absence of a Muslim religious spirituality.

Third and finally, Muslim attitudes have interacted with higher levels of MER in Iranian army and air force military academy cadets to predict not only lower emotional empathy but also lower scores on Islamic Ethical Principles and Universality and on Islamic Duty, Obligation, and Exclusivism Scales (Abu Raiya et al. 2008). When MER was lower, Muslim attitudes displayed a direct association with Islamic ethical principles, a slightly inverse connection with Islamic duty, and a less strong though clearly negative linkage with emotional empathy (Ghorbani, Watson, Asadi, and Chen 2018). These unexpected effects in military cadets perhaps identified a potential for Muslim religious spirituality to support a release from empathic and ideological controls if demanded by military circumstances. More generally, these data also revealed that a Muslim religious spirituality may have role-specific implications that deserve further analysis (Ghorbani, Watson, Geranmayepour, and Chen 2014a).

3.5   Greater Jihad in Pakistan

In popular consciousness, the word 'jihad' means 'holy war' for the understandable reason that the media use this concept to describe Muslim terrorism. Unsurprisingly, however, Muslim meanings of jihad are more complex; and that complexity suggests a need to return to previously mentioned controversies over how to explain the violence of the Thirty Years' War in the West (Cavanaugh 2009). While some narratives argue that Reformation bloodshed was the cause that produced modernism as the effect and solution to the problem of religious violence, a careful reading of the historical record supports the alternative narrative that political discord in the West used religion as a violent tool for producing modernist political arrangements as an effect. A useful oversimplification would be that it was not religion that radically transformed politics but rather politics that radically transformed religion.

A similar story could also be told about jihad as holy war. Specifically, it was not that a careful reading of Muslim texts and traditions radically transformed politics but rather that political factors radically transformed the reading of Muslim texts and traditions. The Arabic root for jihad is *jahada* and denotes the struggle associated with the "putting forth of great effort to achieve a goal" (Kaltner 2011, p. 166). A prominent meaning of that great effort came to be holy war as Muslims confronted struggles against outside political powers. Those problems began centuries ago in conflicts with British colonialism on the Indian subcontinent. Within that political climate, the turn toward to jihad as holy war made sense along with a turn away from "*aman*, or the granting of peace to non-Muslims" (Jalal 2008, p. 15).

More contemporary manifestations of holy war display parallel interpretative possibilities. Mekhennet (2017) examined recent jihadi activity in a method that included dialogues with figures active in the movement. Interesting in her initial dialogue with one ISIS member who had grown up in Europe was his explanation of his own motivations: "In Europe, look how we have been treated ... I wanted to be in the society I grew up with, but I felt, 'You're just the Muslim, you're just the Moroccan, you will never be accepted'" (Mekhennet, p. 4). He also mentioned the American invasion of Iraq in the absence of weapons of mass destruction and the humiliations of Abu Ghraib: "Then they're pointing at us and saying how barbaric we are" (Mekhennet, p. 4). In short, he did not imply that readings of Muslim traditions moved him toward holy war but rather that political circumstances in Europe and elsewhere moved him to pursue holy war.

Political factors also explained European reactions to Muslims (Mekhennet 2017). This complicated story will include international political arrangements that resulted in the establishment of Israel as a state followed by Palestinian resistance. Among other things, the Israeli-Palestinian conflict led, for example, to terrorism at the 1972 Munich Olympics in which Israeli athlete hostages, Palestinian hostage takers, and one policeman died. Events like these encouraged the reactive isolation of Muslim communities within Europe that then led to the alienation and radicalization of Muslim youth and eventual jihadists in a self-reinforcing cycle. Mekhennet (2017) argues that "Western societies and politicians have made little progress toward addressing the policies that radicalize [these] young men" (p. 6). She later adds the more general conclusion, "Religion doesn't radicalize people; people radicalize religion" (Mekhemmet, p. 318). The implication in ISM paraphrase is, therefore "Religion doesn't radicalize politics; politics radicalizes religion."

More broadly, jihad as holy war can find no easy warrant in spiritual meanings sanctioned by Muslim traditions (Jalal 2008; Kaltner 2011). The term holy war, for example, cannot be found in the Qur'an. The Qur'an does refer to *jihad fi sabil allah*, but this means "jihad in the way of God. But even these verses ... are typically followed by exhortations to patience in adversity and leniency in strength, the essence of being of gentle disposition" (Jallal, p. 7). Additional spiritual meanings appear in the hadith, which is a collection of sayings related to the Prophet Mohammad. In one hadith entry, the Prophet defends his community by beating back a military attack and calls this struggle the "lesser war," or *jihad al-asghar*. The lesser jihad, he then goes on to argue, is necessary in order "to fight the *jihad al-akbar*, or the greater war, against those base inner forces which prevent man from becoming human in accordance with his primordial and God-given nature" (Jalal, p. 9). For some, therefore, jihad in Islam does not support holy war. Rather, the lesser jihad of defensive warfare is a sometimes-necessary expediency that leads to the profoundly more important greater jihad against inner forces that interfere with a Muslim's submission to God.

Intra-ideological conflicts in how God as the ultimate standard should be viewed will at least partially explain why some Muslims embrace jihad as holy war whereas others emphasize the greater jihad instead. Given the problem of incommensurability, these somewhat nonempirical ultimate standards will resist rational or social scientific adjudication. On the other hand, beliefs in the greater jihad will mean that operationalization of this construct should confirm its validity within Muslim communities, a goal accomplished in a recent study that developed a Greater Jihad Scale in Pakistan (Khan, Watson, Ali, and Chen, forthcoming).

Underlying the Greater Jihad Scale was the assumption that this construct should express the struggle of an individual with *nafs*. Abu Raiya (2012, 2014) describes *nafs* as elements within traditional Islamic conceptualizations of the personality that usually tend toward evil. They include *nafs ammarah besoa'*, reflecting the evil-inducing influences of instinctual desires that roughly correspond to the id in Freud's (1923/1990) structural model, and *al-nafs al-lawammah*, operating as a reproachful conscience in rough parallel with the superego of Freud. Tensions between instincts and conscience place the individual in recurrent states of psychological discomfort. The *a'ql* is somewhat like the ego of Freud's structural model in that it works as a mediator between instincts, morality, and the demands of reality, but the *a'ql* also differs from the Freudian ego in that it includes an angelic dimension that works to bring conflicts among these forces into a submission to God. The rare achievement of this full submission occurs with the serenity of *al-nafs al-mutmainnah*.

Potential Greater Jihad Scale items essentially sought to record struggles of the individual to strengthen the *a'ql*. An Islamic scholar called an *alim* with expertise in *sharia* law listed possible expressions of the Greater Jihad, and two other individuals experienced in reading the *Qur'an* and the hadith further evaluated and refined those items. Administration of these statements along with a number of psychological and religious scales then occurred with samples of Pakistani university and madrassa religious school students. Expressions of the greater jihad defined two factors. A 5-item Societal Jihad measure included such self-reports as "The Greater Jihad against *nafs* is very important for the correction of society" and "Society can never be clean or correct till all of us can perform the Greater Jihad." Indicative of the 6-item Self-Jihad factor were the statements, "The Greater Jihad requires that I have to sacrifice my personal desires and wishes" and "In the Greater Jihad, I find it difficult to fight against those actions that are not allowed in Islam."

Madrassa students scored higher on the Greater Jihad Scale than did university students as would be expected for a variable that putatively reflects stronger commitments to Islam. Some complexities did appear in correlations with other measures across the two samples, but overall relationships most importantly revealed that the Greater Jihad constructs correlated positively with each other and with the intrinsic religious orientation, satisfaction with life, and a broader measure of Islamic moral values (Francis, Sahin, and

Al-Failakawi 2008). In short, the Greater Jihad predicted Muslim religious and psychological adjustment.

These Greater Jihad data had two especially noteworthy implications. First, the Greater Jihad prediction of greater life satisfaction may be at least somewhat paradoxical relative to assumptions that dominate Western psychology. One Societal Jihad item asserted, for instance, "I feel guilty when I am not able to act according to the Greater Jihad," whereas one self-report of Self Jihad said, "The Greater Jihad requires that I have to sacrifice my personal desires and wishes." In the West, the expectation would likely be that guilt and a sacrifice of personal desires would predict less rather than more life satisfaction. These results, therefore, supported the specific suggestions of Smither and Khorsandi (2009), "One of the greatest areas of difference between most approaches to personality and Islam is the Islamic belief in the overall beneficence of society and the importance of subordinating one's personal desires for what is seen as the greater good" (p. 92).

On the other hand, emphasis might also be placed on parallels that seem evident between American Christian beliefs in sin and Pakistani Muslim understandings of the greater jihad. Again, Christian sin-related beliefs include such self-reports as "Nobody in the world is really good, least of all, am I" and perhaps surprisingly, predict better mental health (Watson, Morris, and Hood 1988a, 1988b, 1989). Findings that Western Christian and Pakistani Muslim subordinations of the self can describe psychological adjustment suggest that broader philosophical and not just Islam-specific considerations are relevant here.

Sorokin's (1941/1992) analysis of freedom may point toward one useful interpretative framework. He analyzed freedom in terms of a ratio involving personal satisfactions divided by personal desires. This ratio makes it clear that freedom can increase in two ways. What he called sensate freedom increases as long as satisfactions grow at a higher rate than desires. Sensate freedom would essentially define modernist freedoms in, for example, democratic political and capitalist economic social arrangements. Ascetic freedom would appear instead as desires become lower relative to available satisfactions. At the extreme, a religious believer would seek to desire only God, and an increasing awareness of all the blessings that God had made available as satisfactions would enhance the experience of freedom. In other words, theist freedom is ascetic freedom.

Conceptualizations of freedom and thus of mental health are ideological. Sorokin's analysis does not formally suggest a definition of Nietzschean freedom which presumably operates as an unbridled pursuit of desire that uses the will to power to obtain satisfactions spontaneously in the present. But the conclusion seems clear. Any attempts to evaluate theist psychological functioning relative to modernist or Nietzschean understandings of freedom might yield insights but would also reflect ideological rather than 'objective' frames of reference. Theist researchers should operationalize their own traditions so that they can more deeply appreciate the adjustment benefits of ascetic freedom.

Greater Jihad data may have a second more important implication. All religions will have negative potentials that need to be addressed. According to the ISM, such problems require a methodological theism that offers an increasingly holistic operationalization of an entire religious tradition and that expresses intra-ideological resources for bringing the normative assumptions of a social rationality into better conformity with the perceived demands of its ultimate standard. The greater jihad may have that potential relative to what some argue are the more questionable normative assumptions associated with jihad as holy war (Jalal 2008). Interactions between religious and nonreligious traditions then need to work toward the common good by 'truthfully' and 'objectively' understanding the strengths and weaknesses of all social rationalities as they seek to socially construct a more humane public space. Resistances to methodological theism may, therefore, need to be informed by a realization that the issues are not limited to epistemological social scientific concerns but apply more importantly to the challenges of social life in a pluralistic world. Methodological theism will make invaluable contributions to resolving those challenges and should never be ignored.

3.6   Broader Conclusions about the Operationalization of Traditions

ISM efforts to operationalize religious traditions have at least seven broader implications beyond the more specific suggestions of the Greater Jihad data. First, to reemphasize the central point, efforts to operationalize and then analyze religious traditions document the potentials of methodological theism. Methodological atheism cannot study the ultimate standard of Nature taken as a whole just as methodological theism cannot study the ultimate standard of a Christian or a Muslim God taken as a whole. Each incommensurable social rationality can and should respond to its own somewhat nonempirical ultimate standard by using research methods to analyze the normative regularities that exist in the organization of its derivative inferences. Religious and non-religious research participants can serve as informants about the normative impact of Nature. Religious research participants can also serve as informants about the normative impact of their visions of God. Studies examining sin and grace in American Christians, religious spirituality in Iranian Muslims, and the Greater Jihad in Pakistani Muslims make it clear that methodological theism is like methodological atheism in having potentials for psychometric objectivity and for promoting insights into the psychology of religiousness.

Second, methodological theism can enrich social rationalities within a religious tradition. Findings that Self-Improvement might be central in explaining linkages of sin-related beliefs with Christian adjustment and that Healthy Humility might at least sometimes be unhealthy need to be replicated and extended (Watson et al. 2007). Confirmation of these outcomes could encourage a deeper biblical analysis of the relevant issues, and this could lead to a more reflective and insightful Christian social rationality. Therapists and counselors who frame their practice within a Christian ideological surround presumably would also find it useful to better understand the dynamics of Self-Improvement and Healthy Humility within their clients' sin-related beliefs. Demonstrations that the spirituality of a close and loving submission to God may incite, integrate, and invigorate Muslim religious commitments could also be important in encouraging more reflective developments in the theory and practice of Islamic social rationality.

Third, success in operationalizing one religious tradition could encourage additional research in that and in other religious traditions. A more wholistic rather than an atomistic analysis of religion and spirituality in Iran has led, for example, to the formulation of a 3-I Model that offers a preliminary heuristic framework for understanding religious spirituality. This model may or may not prove to be fruitful in the long run; but regardless of eventual outcome, research into the model across religious traditions has a potential to encourage a broader understanding of the psychology of religion and spirituality. Even falsifications of the model could usefully clarify spirituality.

Fourth, methodological theism can challenge anti-psychological theists who reject the methods of contemporary psychology as a contamination of what should instead be an exclusively biblical analysis of the person (Powlison 2010). Potential problems with this rejection may appear in findings that Self-Improvement may explain the mental health benefits of Christian sin-related beliefs and that Healthy Humility can be unhealthy. All four Beliefs about Sin presumably can find warrant within the Bible. So, biblically speaking, how can Healthy Humility sometimes be unhealthy; and why were Perfectionism Avoidance and Self-Reflective Functioning relatively unimportant in predicting Christian adjustment? Anti-psychological theists can perhaps find biblical explanations for such outcomes, but how would they even know of the need to do so in the absence of empirical evidence?

Fifth, anti-psychological theists might merely choose to ignore findings like those observed with the Beliefs about Sin Scale by simply reaffirming a narrative that emphasizes the need to wall out all social scientific empiricism. Counter-arguments against that narrative would likely lead to interminable and unproductive conflicts across essentially incommensurable social rationalities. On the other hand, methodological theists could use empirical methods to analyze the pronouncements of anti-psychological theists. Discoveries of a poor correspondence between those pronouncements and even informal observations of Christian social life would point toward a process of ghettoization that moved anti-psychological theism away from authoritativeness toward a presumably problematic authoritarianism.

Sixth, the operationalization of religious traditions may have important implications for methodological atheism. Methodological atheists will likely have all kinds of ideological reasons for dismissing Christian beliefs about sin and grace, but it would be a strange kind of 'objectivity' that refused to even consider and then dismiss the empirical realities of those beliefs as documented by methodological theism. Methodological atheists may also have all kinds of ideological reasons for defending an atomistic approach to the study of religion and spirituality. At the same time, however, it would be a strange kind of 'objectivity' that refused to assess whether indices of generic spirituality in the West can produce 3-I effects equivalent to those observed with a Muslim religious spirituality. Demonstrations that generic measures produced equivalent 3-I effects would strengthen atomistic interpretations of spirituality, whereas failures of such scales to produce equivalent effects could suggest interpretative problems that required further analysis. Either way, objectivity in the understanding of spirituality by methodological atheists would seem to require some kind of interaction with findings made available by methodological theists.

Seventh and finally, the methodological theist operationalization of traditions represents no social scientific threat to methodological atheism. As interpreted by the ISM, methodological theism in league with metaphysical theism reflects an incommensurable social rationality that can in no way falsify the incommensurable social rationality of methodological atheism in league with metaphysical atheism, and vice versa. Advocates of each could choose to explain away the findings of the other simply by further developing their own triumphalist monologues. Even a triumphalist atheism, therefore, might, benefit from developments in methodological theism, just as a triumphalist theism might benefit from developments in methodological atheism. This is so because the triumphalist narratives of both could become more complex; although, tendencies toward authoritarianism would also increase in the absence of formal empirical dialogues.

3.7 *Resistances*

In a reflection of its own originating social rationality, the ISM advocates methodological and metaphysical theism and the operationalization of religious traditions as an ideological commitment to 'truth' and 'objectivity' (Watson 2006, 2011). This 'truth' and 'objectivity' will require an awareness that social rationalities will be organized around diverse ultimate standards and that they consequently will be incommensurable. In the absence of this awareness, authoritarianism becomes a temptation. For authoritarians, others who refuse to submit to the logic of what unreflectively seems to be the obvious master rationality must be saved from their own ignorance, irrationality, or sinfulness through some exercise of the will to power. Turns toward Power reflect steps toward betrayals of the ultimate standards of God or of Nature. Against such temptations, the ISM recommends the social scientific and broader cultural development of dialogue as a way forward. Ideological disagreements define a public space in which monological rationalities frequently talk and sometimes scream past each other. Public space requires instead the development of an increasingly sophisticated dialogical rationality.

But of course, no master rationality will be available for compelling any social rationality to embrace dialogue as a derivative inference. This will be most obvious for triumphalist theists and triumphalist atheists. Even some methodological theists and atheists will be sympathetic to the need for dialogue, but so much will need to be done that they understandably will only focus on how to operationalize their own traditions as a way to deepen their own social rationalities. Such tendencies will work against the ability of procedures to operationalize religious traditions to expand dialogue across religious and social scientific rationalities. The ISM, therefore, pursues additional methodological innovations that seek to document the necessity of attending to rather than ignoring ideological factors in relationships between psychology and religion. Those procedures can be described as a theist methodological dialogism.

4 Theist Methodological Dialogism

All kinds of factors will explain why the rationalities of psychology in understanding religion will ignore the rationalities of religion in understanding psychology and vice versa. No master rationality will be available for developing compelling arguments for a dialogue between psychology and religion and against the triumphalisms that can exist within each. Incommensurability will mean that any such arguments will have no access to a noncontroversial shared standard of adjudication that can 'objectively' resolve disagreements.

Conflicts between the two will consequently have a potential to be interminable and unproductive.

In response to this problem, the ISM claims that 'objectivity' in the study of psychology and religion will require not only an awareness of the trials associated with incommensurability but also an empirical analysis of its dialogical implications. Procedures that operationalize psychological and religious traditions have a potential to promote that awareness, but they too will have limitations. In part, this will be so because the triumphalism of one ideological surround will promote a ghettoization that walls out the understandings of other ideological surrounds. In addition, the daunting challenges of operationalizing one tradition will take away for the time required to develop sophisticated understandings other social rationalities.

On the other hand, direct empirical demonstrations that ideology can influence psychological as well as religious ideological surrounds may be more difficult to ignore for social rationalities committed to 'truth.' The ISM tries to make this clear through development of a theist methodological dialogism that works against ghettoization by bringing incommensurable psychological and religious rationalities into direct dialogue. Methodological dialogism does not naively assume that disagreements among incommensurable rationalities can be resolved harmoniously through dialogue. The hope instead is that interminable arguments at the intersections of psychology and religion can be made more productive.

4.1 Psychometric Deconstruction of Psychometrics

Theist methodological dialogisms bring derivative inferences of social rationalities rather than their incommensurable ultimate standards into direct interactions adjudicated by social scientific standards of reliability and validity. The overall process essentially operates as a kind of empirical hermeneutics. More specifically, methodological dialogisms bring the psychometric expressions of norms associated with one ideological surround into some interpretative relationship with the normative assumptions of a different ideological surround. Significant findings in the analysis of such relationships would operate as a psychometric deconstruction of psychometrics and would confirm that 'objectivity' requires a sensitivity to how ideology can taint measures used in the study of psychology and religion. Three preliminary considerations deserve emphasis.

First, methodological dialogism is an option available across all ideological surrounds. Because of the originating commitments of the ISM (Watson 2006), development of these procedures has occurred as an exercise in a theist methodological dialogism committed to metaphysical theism. An atheist methodological dialogism in league with metaphysical atheism would be possible as well. Methodological dialogism might also examine intersections between two different religions or between two different perspectives within a single religion. Each of these procedures would empirically evaluate the possibility of psychometrically based violations of 'truthfulness' in the understandings that exist within and between ideological surrounds.

Second, methodological dialogisms can work against tendencies toward extremist differentiations between ideological surrounds. Triumphalists will presume the unassailable rationality of their home monologue and the thorough-going irrationality of other ideological surrounds. Demonstrations of incompatibilities between home and outside derivative inferences will tend to support that thinking. Methodological dialogisms, however, will document compatibilities and irrelevancies across ideological surrounds, and along with data related to the operationalization of traditions, such outcomes will work toward more judicious interactions between social rationalities.

Third, efforts to develop a theist methodological dialogism have been primarily illustrative. The overriding ISM goal has been to explore as many methodological innovations as possible for demonstrating ideological influences within research programs examining psychology and religion. Better and more sensitive methods of dialogue may well be developed in the future. Previous findings will also need to be replicated and extended before they can be accepted as definitive. These important caveats should be kept in mind when examining the five ISM methodological innovations illustrated thus far.

4.2 *Direct Rational Analysis*

The simplest method of dialogism is direct rational analysis. With this procedure, a researcher rationally evaluates items within a measure that operationalizes the derivative inferences of one social rationality relative to the ultimate standard of a different social rationality. Items could be interpreted as compatible, incompatible, or neutral relative to the outside ideological surround. Deconstruction of the initial scale into ideologically differentiated components would then produce measures for examination in correlations with other constructs. Patterns of those correlations would clarify the possibility of ideological influences built into the original instrument.

Use of this procedure has occurred with a psychological scale expressing derivative inferences associated with an existential ideological surround (Watson, Hood and Morris 1988). This Avoidance of Existential Confrontation Scale (AECS) attempts to assess psychologically damaging efforts to deny the harsher realities of life (Thauberger and Sydiaha-Symor 1977). Death, suffering, and meaninglessness are among those harsher realities. In a largely Christian sample, the AECS correlated positively with both the intrinsic religious orientation and with a measure of dispositional anxiety. Data reflecting this existential ideological surround, therefore, supported the possibility that sincere religious commitments moved Christians toward anxiety-producing denials of the disturbing realities of life.

Possible ideological influences, nevertheless, seemed obvious within the AECS. This scale expressed an avoidance of existential confrontation in the self-reports that "God exists" and that it is "quite certain what happens after death." Both beliefs reflect prominent Christian and other theist derivative inferences. A direct rational analysis, therefore, subdivided the AECS into ideologically distinct religious (AECS-R) and nonreligious (AECS-N) subscales. The AECS-R displayed a strong positive relationship with the intrinsic religious orientation and a nonsignificant tendency to predict *lower* rather than higher anxiety. The AECS-N instead exhibited no relationship with the intrinsic religious orientation and a robust positive linkage with anxiety. A psychometric deconstruction of the AECS, therefore, confirmed that that full-scale data had problematic implications for religious commitments because of anti-religious ideological presumptions built into this operationalization of an existential ideological surround.

4.3 *Correlational Marker Analysis*

Correlational marker analyses of a psychological scale move the dialogical processes of ideological hermeneutical interpretation away from the researcher conducting a direct rational analysis toward the research participants themselves. In this procedure, participants receive a measure to be dialogically 'clarified' along with a 'marker' scale that has well established validity as an index of religious commitments. Correlations of the 'marker' with each item within the 'clarified' instrument will identify derivative inferences that are compatible, incompatible, or neutral within a religious social rationality. Correlations of these subsets of items with other measures can then assess the possibility of ideological influences built into the 'clarified' instrument.

In one use of this procedure, the Intrinsic Religious Orientation Scale served as a marker for clarifying self-actualization as expressed within a humanistic ideological surround (Watson, Morris and Hood 1989). A largely Christian sample responded to a 150-item operationalization of humanistic self-actualization (Shostrom 1974). Positive correlations with the intrinsic religious orientation uncovered Pro-Christian humanistic derivative inferences, but negative correlations pointed instead toward Anti-Christian beliefs. Illustrating a Pro-Christian belief was the self-report that "I do not have feelings of resentment about things that are past," a result presumably reflecting

Christian beliefs in forgiveness (e.g., Matthew 6:14–15). Anti-Christian beliefs appeared, for instance, in the assertion that "people need not repent their wrongdoings." This need for repentance in Christian understandings of sin has already been explained. Pro-Christian statements combined into a single measure predicted better mental health, whereas Anti-Christian items pointed toward poorer psychological functioning as made evident in correlations with other measures. Perhaps most importantly, however, Pro-Christian and Anti-Christian subscales correlated negatively. This psychometric deconstruction of a humanistic index of self-actualization unmasked an otherwise hidden violation of the basic psychometric standard of internal reliability. This humanistic scale, therefore, was at least somewhat incoherent ideologically.

Correlational marker procedures, therefore, can document problematic interactions between psychology and religion, but other possibilities exist as well. In a largely American Christian sample, positive correlations with the intrinsic religious orientation revealed that 15 out of 36 items from a Self-Control Scale (Tangney, Baumeister, and Boone 2004) defined a Christian Self-Control subscale (Watson and Morris 2008). Christian Self-Control correlated positively with the more neutral Non-Christian items, and both generally predicted mental health with some minor contrasts in the pattern of their linkages with other variables. Christian Self-Control also included Behavioral Control, Impulse Control, and Disciplined Consistency factors. Disciplined Consistency was the only factor to *reliably* predict Christian adjustment, thus confirming its validity as in fact more *consistently* disciplined. Average responding on the Christian Self-Control items was also higher than on the Non-Christian items, with this result further confirming the validity of this dialogical differentiation between Christian and Non-Christian Self-Control. Overall, these data made it clear that correlational marker procedures can be useful not only in clarifying incompatibilities between psychology and religion, but also in encouraging deeper appreciations of the compatibilities that can also exist between them.

4.4 *Comparative Rationality Analysis*

With direct rationality analysis, the ISM pursues a hermeneutical empiricism by bringing religious norms as interpreted by a researcher into dialogue with a psychological scale that expresses normative derivative inferences of a different ideological surround. With correlational marker procedures, the research participants themselves, rather than the researcher, indirectly supply the hermeneutical fulcrum of analysis through their responses to a scale that 'marks' their religious commitment. Comparative rationality analysis (CRA) moves the process one step further along by having the research participants directly rather than indirectly supply the religious interpretative framework.

In CRA procedures, research participants respond to a psychological scale twice. First, they react to the items of an instrument as administered and eventually scored under standard instructions. Later, they respond to these very same items once again, but this time, they evaluate each in terms of its degree of inconsistency or consistency with personal religious beliefs. Those evaluations will then make it possible to examine the full scale in a 'macro-rationality analysis' and each individual item in a 'micro-rationality analysis.'

Macro-rationality analyses sum religious consistency ratings of all items into a total score that quantitatively expresses the religious interpretation of a scale by the sample. Full scale and macro-rationality scores will then correlate positively if sample religiousness systematically affects responding, and the strength of that relationship will suggest the magnitude of the ideological influence. Positive correlations between scales and ratings will appear regardless of whether evaluations across items are generally inconsistent or generally consistent with religious commitments. Higher scores of religious participants on a construct like self-control, for example, should be accompanied by higher religious consistency ratings. Conversely, lower scores on a construct like dispositional depression should be accompanied by lower religious consistency ratings. In each instance, lower scores will predict lower scores, and higher scores will predict higher scores. Positive correlations, therefore, will not reveal whether the ideological perspectives of the full scale and the sample are compatible or incompatible. An examination of how these two measures correlate with other variables will be necessary to make that determination.

In procedures recently explained in greater detail elsewhere (Watson, Chen, Morris, and Ghorbani 2017), micro-rationality analyses evaluate each item within an instrument separately so that the scale as administered under standard instructions can eventually be rescored, if necessary, according to the religious ideological interpretations of the sample. Items evaluated as 'neutral' would be ignored in these rescoring procedures. 'Pro-religious' items would remain scored as in the original measure, but 'antireligious' items would be rescored in an opposite direction to make them compatible with the sample religious ideological surround. Comparative analyses of these two scoring methods in relationships with other measures would then assess their relative validity.

Gradual evolution of CFA procedures occurred across years of research that examined ideological presumptions built into an early form of cognitive psychotherapy (Watson 2010). Rational-emotive therapy (RET) was the initial name given this cognitive therapy by its founder Albert Ellis (1962). CFA procedures early in this research program were not as sophisticated as they were later, but the overall conclusions remained clear throughout.

RET rests upon an A-B-C model of psychopathology in which activating (A) life events presumably produce disturbed psychological consequences (C) only through the mediation of irrational beliefs (B). For Ellis, religious beliefs were especially disturbing irrationalities. It was he, for example, who offered the previously mentioned assertion that the "concept of sin is the direct and indirect cause of virtually all neurotic disturbance" (Ellis 1962, p. 146). More generally, he argued that religiosity "is in many respects equivalent to irrational thinking and emotional disturbance.... The elegant therapeutic solution to emotional problems is to be quite unreligious and have no degree of dogmatic faith that is unfounded or unfoundable in fact" (Ellis 1980, p. 637). About all persons, he concluded, therefore, "The less religious they are, the more emotionally healthy they will be" (Ellis 1980, p. 637).

Behind RET is an assumption that rationality can be described for entire populations without any concern about ideologographic influences. CFA tests of this hypothesis supported at least five conclusions (see Watson 2010; Watson et al. 1994). First, what RET identified as a therapeutic irrationality sometimes proved to be a religious rationality. A dependency scale, for example, recorded an RET irrationality that included such theistic beliefs as the idea that "people need a source of strength outside themselves" (e.g., Psalms 23:1–3). CFA procedure documented this index of dependency as a religious rationality that predicted psychological adjustment rather than maladjustment. Second, other putative irrationalities like perfectionism included a complex mix of neutral, anti-religious, and pro-religious beliefs. Third, micro-rationality assessments revealed that a majority of RET rationalities were actually religious rationalities. Across a total of 161 RET irrationalities, sincerely religious research participants interpreted 83 as pro-religious, 50 as antireligious, and 28 as neutral. Fourth, comparisons between RET scorings and Christian micro-rationality re-scorings of irrational beliefs supplied evidence that Christian rationality could at least sometimes be more valid when used with Christians. Fifth and most generally, this research program, therefore, demonstrated that ideological factors can indeed influence psychological systems of rationality.

CFA procedures have also examined other psychological constructs, including post-traumatic growth (Andrews et al. 2017), religious problem-solving styles in both Iran (Ghorbani, Watson, Saeedi, Chen, and Silver 2012) and the United States (Watson et al. 2017), and the Dark Triad measures of psychopathy, narcissism, and Machiavellianism (Watson, Chen, Morris, and Ghorbani 2018). All these uses of CRA have made it clear that any dismissal of religion as wholly 'irrational' cannot be 'objective' even within the ideological surrounds of methodological and metaphysical atheism. CFA data demonstrate instead that religions can operate as meaningful and psychologically beneficial social rationalities organized around commitments to the incommensurable ultimate standards associated with visions of God.

Such a conclusion in no way means that CRA procedures have revealed religious rationalities to be without curiosities to be explained. With a deferring problem-solving style, for instance, religious individuals leave it to God to resolve personal difficulties (Pargament et al. 1988). In Iran, micro-rationality scores identified deferring-style items to be consistent, neutral, and inconsistent with religious commitments. A few consistent and mostly neutral items appeared in the United States. Consistent items in Iran predicted psychological adjustment, but inconsistent items unexpectedly described a Muslim maladjustment that seemed more logically reverse-scored as a non-deferring, more 'secular' expression of adjustment reflecting attempts of the individual to solve problems independently of God. That more 'secular' expressions of the deferring style might be psychologically healthier was perhaps an especially surprising outcome in a formally Muslim society like Iran.

In a study of mostly Christian Americans, psychopathy and Machiavellianism macro-rationality scores displayed expected correlations that were negative with the intrinsic religious orientation and positive with psychological maladjustment. Surprisingly, however, micro-rationality analyses found no Dark Triad items to be either inconsistent or consistent with religious commitments. The inability of a more wholistic macro-rationality to be reductively explained by a micro-rationality analysis is a complexity that deserves further analysis. In short, Iranian and American findings illustrate the potentials of CRA to uncover the complexities that can exist within both religious and psychological ideological surrounds and that deserve additional analysis.

4.5 Empirical Translation Schemes

Empirical translations schemes deconstruct a scale that expresses the derivative inferences of one ideological surround by attempting to translate it into the derivative inferences of a different ideological surround (Roth 1987; Watson 2008). In these procedures as most commonly used thus far, research participants respond to a scale that expresses normative functioning within a psychological ideological surround and then they respond to other statements that attempt to express the same ideas in religious language. Positive correlations between psychological and religious expressions of a statement identify a successful translation. Successful translations can then be combined into a religious measure for comparison with the initial scale in relationships with other variables. Those comparisons will bring psychological and religious social rationalities into direct dialogue.

First use of empirical translation schemes examined American Christian concerns about culturally corrupting influences that presumably exist within humanistic psychology (Watson 2008). The humanistic norm of self-actualization, in particular, seemed wholly incompatible with Christian beliefs about a sinful self in need of repentance. Empirical translation schemes questioned that concern when all humanistic expressions of self-actualization within a 10-item scale (Jones and Crandell 1986) were successfully translated into Christian language (Watson et al. 1995). One assertion of humanistic self-actualization said, for instance, "I can like people without having to approve of them." A successful Christian translation said, "Christ's love for sinners has taught me to love people regardless of their background and lifestyle." Successful translations defined an overall Christian Self-Actualization Scale that predicted higher levels of Christian commitment and proved to be more valid that than the humanistic measure in assessing Christian psychological adjustment.

Modifications of empirical translation scheme procedures also made it possible to translate the Budner (1962) Intolerance of Ambiguity Scale into a Christian Tolerance of Ambiguity measure (Watson and Morris 2006). Negative correlations between an original Budner item and a possible translation identified statements that transformed a self-report indicating an inability to cope with uncertainty into one that reflected a Christian embrace of uncertainty. One reverse scored Intolerance of Ambiguity item said, for instance, "Often the most interesting and stimulating people are those who don't mind being different and original," and correlating negatively with this statement was the directly scored self-report, "For me, the most stimulating and interesting Christians are those who have the courage to be different and original just as our Lord was different and original." Intolerance of Ambiguity correlated positively with religious commitments and with more constrained forms of psychological functioning. Christian Tolerance of Ambiguity instead displayed positive correlations with religious commitments and with more open psychological perspectives. An exclusive research focus on Intolerance of Ambiguity would, therefore, have yielded very incomplete and misleading conclusions about Christian commitments and a tolerance of uncertainty. Empirical translation schemes made it possible to offer a more comprehensive and balanced assessment of the issue.

Later empirical translation scheme studies expressed post-traumatic growth (Andrews et al. 2017) in the language of American Christians and translated self-control (Ghorbani, Watson, Tavakoli, and Chen 2016) and mindfulness (Ghorbani, Watson, Tavakoli, and Chen 2018) into the language of Iranian Muslims. Psychological and religious expressions of these constructs displayed largely parallel implications in correlations with other variables. Both psychological and religious expressions of a construct also sometimes combined in multiple regression procedures to explain independent sources of variance in these other measures, suggesting that each made a unique contribution to the prediction of adjustment.

Further clarifications of psychological and religious expressions of the same construct can be accomplished by using both as simultaneous mediators (Baron and Kenny 1986) in two sets of causal models (Andrews et al. 2017; Ghorbani, Watson, Tavakoli, and Chen 2016, 2018). In one set of models, a psychological construct serves as the independent variable with the dependent variables being both psychological and religious scales. In another set, the independent variable is a measure of religious functioning with the dependent variables once again being indices of psychological and religious functioning. Numerous outcomes are theoretically possible. Only the psychological or only the religious expression of a variable might be a significant mediator. Mediation might instead be an ideologically specific process in which a psychological mediator only explained relationships between of psychological independent and dependent variables, and only the religious translation mediated linkages between religious independent and dependent variables. Alternatively, ideologically general mediation processes might appear when both psychological and religious mediators explained relationships between both psychological and religious independent and dependent variables. Although complexities can appear, these analyses most importantly reveal that ideologically general mediation effects can appear.

Perhaps most importantly, these studies demonstrate that broad compatibilities can exist between psychological and religious social rationalities. Any psychological dismissal of religion as wholly irrational and any religious dismissal of psychology as wholly inimical to faith, therefore, need to be examined with empirical translation schemes. Data obtained thus far suggest that presumed incompatibilities might at least sometimes represent opportunities to use empirical translation schemes for empirically constructing a common ground between psychological and religious social rationalities.

4.6   *Statistical Controls for Ideology*

One final procedure of a theist methodological dialogism has involved the use of statistical controls to tease apart the influences of ideology on research outcomes. Underlying this procedure is an assumption that the somewhat nonempirical influences of ideology can obscure relationships between measures expressing psychological and theist ideological surrounds. Statistical controls make it possible to test this hypothesis. These procedures also make it possible to examine ideological complexities that can exist within a single religious tradition.

First use of these procedures occurred with a largely Christian American sample and involved an analysis of self-adjustment as understood within theist and humanist ideological surrounds (Watson, Morris, and Hood 1987). Research participants responded to scales recording various aspects of their religious commitments and to self-functioning measures that assessed self-acceptance, self-esteem, and self-actualization. Religious commitments displayed four linkages with maladjustment, one correlation with adjustment, and an overwhelming majority of 25 relationships that were nonsignificant. Included among these measures were scales that assessed religious beliefs about sin and guilt that were clearly anti-humanistic in their ideological implications and self-actualization as expressed in humanistic terms that were clearly anti-religious. Partial correlations 'subtracted' out the influences of these anti-humanistic and anti-religious languages and revealed that religious commitments no longer predicted any form of maladjustment and instead displayed 20 positive and 10 nonsignificant associations with mental health. The suggestion, therefore, was that ideological presumptions built into the languages of religion and humanistic psychology obscured the compatibilities that may exist between them.

Other uses of statistical control procedures have been combined with empirical translation schemes to document ideological complexities within Christian traditions. Development of the Religious Fundamentalism Scale occurred within a psychological research program that sought assess the psychosocially problematic consequences of maintaining commitments to the fundamentals of a religious faith (Altemeyer and Hunsberger 1992, 2004; Hunsberger 1996). Among other things, this scale assumes that fundamentalists believe that God is "opposed by forces of evil which must be vigorously fought" (Altemeyer and Hunsberger 1992, p. 118). One item says, for example, "The basic cause of evil in this world is Satan, who is still constantly and ferociously fighting against God." American Christian fundamentalists, therefore, appear to find themselves embattled in a culture war against Satan (e.g., Hunter 1991).

Within the ISM, however, the concern is whether Religious Fundamentalism might fail to capture more adjusted potentials within Christian commitments to fundamentals. Explorations of that possibility used empirical translation schemes to transform a Religious Fundamentalism engaged in a culture war against Satan into a Biblical Foundationalism more strongly organized around visions of a loving and nurturing God as the ultimate standard (Watson et al. 2003). Religious Fundamentalism items can also suggest an ideological splitting in which those within the faith are all good and those outside the faith are all bad. Biblical Foundationalism translations attempted to avoid this splitting.

In short, Biblical Foundationalism sought to express a more loving and less splitting commitment to religious fundamentals. One Religious Fundamentalism item said, for instance, "God has given humanity a complete, unfailing guide to happiness and salvation, which must be totally followed," whereas the more loving Biblical Foundationalist version said, "We should accept the Bible as God's gift to us to follow completely so that we can achieve the peace and salvation that he desires for us." A reverse scored self-report of Religious Fundamentalism was, "Whenever science and sacred scripture conflict, science is probably right." The less splitting Biblical Foundationalist translation said instead, "God's hand is in all creation and in all truth; so, conflicts between faith and science should not frighten us, but rather should inspire us to seek God's truth." The less splitting Biblical Foundationalist translation of the previous mentioned Religious Fundamentalist belief about Satan said, "By taking seriously the biblical stories of Satan, God's true followers will admit the potential reality of evil in themselves and in the world, and this will encourage them to constantly fight against Satan and Satan's allies on this earth."

Religious Fundamentalism and Biblical Foundationalism displayed strong positive correlations. Isolation of their ideological implications, nevertheless, becomes possible through statistical controls that examine Religious Fundamentalism after partialing out Biblical Foundationalism and vice versa. Studies analyzing a wide range of issues have yielded numerous demonstrations that partial correlations for Biblical Foundationalism predict better and partial correlations for Religious Fundamentalism predict poorer psychological functioning. Biblical Foundationalism also exhibits a higher average response per item than Religious Fundamentalism, suggesting that it more strongly reflects the Christian ultimate standard (e.g., Watson, Chen, Ghorbani, and Vartanian 2015; Watson, Chen, and Morris 2014; Watson, Chen, Morris, and Stephenson 2015). Statistical controls for ideology, therefore, suggest that Christian commitments to the fundamentals of their faith may have more positive potentials that deserve further analysis.

4.7 *Conclusions*

Theist methodological dialogisms use the normative assumptions of religious traditions to empirically deconstruct measures that reflect both psychological and religious ideological surrounds. That deconstruction in no way reflects a capitulation to a disintegrative relativism. Deconstruction instead operates as a process of construction in perhaps two most noteworthy ways.

First, theist methodological dialogism displays constructive possibilities for methodological and metaphysical atheism. Direct rational analysis, correlational marker, CFA, empirical translation scheme, and statistical control procedures make it clear that a theist methodological dialogism can identify imprecisions in how atheisms characterize religions and define themselves. Explicit rejections of religious perspectives, for example, may seem integral in efforts to operationalize aspects of non-religious psychological traditions like those expressed in the AECS and in some measures of self-actualization. A psychometric deconstruction of these instruments, nevertheless, demonstrates that at least some of these explicit rejections are empirically unwarranted. The suggestion of the ISM, therefore, is that methodological and metaphysical atheists should encourage theist methodological dialogisms as useful in the maturation rather than the ghettoization of their own social rationalities. 'Objectivity' seems to require it.

More broadly, psychometric deconstructions of psychometrics make it clear that methodological and metaphysical theist programs of research have constructive contributions to make within the overall study of psychology and religion. Theist methodological dialogisms demonstrate, for instance, that triumphalist atheisms, methodological atheisms, methodological agnosticisms, and non-metaphysical empiricisms may inadequately appreciate the empirical impact of metaphysical perspectives on the normative assumptions of psychological as well as religious ideological surrounds. Theist methodological dialogisms also point toward potentials for ghettoization within anti-psychological theisms and indeed within all triumphalisms. Even religious synthesizers, who work to assimilate psychological perspectives within a religious worldview, may maintain a too passive relationship with the discipline of psychology. Sometimes the task is not just to integrate psychology into religion but to critique it as well. Within a pluralist cultural context, research programs committed to theist methodological dialogism seem essential for the maturation of both theist and psychological social rationalities.

5   Religious Openness Hypothesis

Use of empirical translation schemes to express self-control and mindfulness within an Iranian Muslim ideological surround serve as just one illustration of how theist methodological dialogism is not just about methodological innovations but also about the need to bring other religious traditions into the dialogue (Ghorbani, Watson, Tavakoli, and Chen 2016, 2018). Further support for this suggestion appears in recent reexaminations of well-established findings that conservative religiosity can predict psychological and social closed-mindedness in the West (e.g., Altemeyer and Hunsberger 1992; Batson et al. 1993). In combination with other ISM procedures, dialogues across religious traditions have led to a Religious Openness Hypothesis, which argues that conservative religious commitments also have potentials for promoting psychosocial openness (e.g., Ghorbani, Watson, Sarmast, and Chen 2018; Watson, Chen, Ghorbani, and Vartanian 2015).

5.1 Faith and Intellect Oriented Reflection

Initial steps toward this hypothesis began with a study that modified a Religious Reflection Scale created with Muslims in Australia and Malaysia (Dover, Miner, and Dowson 2007) for use with American Christians (Watson, Chen, and Hood 2011). A factor analysis of this modified instrument uncovered two dimensions of Christian Religious Reflection. Indicative of Faith Oriented Reflection was the claim, "Faith in Christ is what nourishes the intellect and makes the intellectual life prosperous and productive." Illustrating Intellect Oriented Reflection were such self-reports as, "I believe as humans we should use our minds to explore all fields of thought from science to metaphysics." A negative linkage between these two factors and their associations with other religious constructs supported the previous literature in depicting conservative religiousness as antithetical to intellectual openness. Three other lines of evidence, nevertheless, revealed such a conclusion to be too simplistic.

First, ideological factors within this initial American sample determined whether Faith Oriented Reflection had closed-minded or open-minded implications (Watson et al. 2011). Previously mentioned statistical controls examined a more maladjusted Religious Fundamentalist ideological surround by using partial correlations to control for Biblical Foundationalism and a more adjusted Biblical Foundationalist surround by using partial correlations to control for Religious Fundamentalism. Faith and Intellect Oriented Reflection displayed a negative linkage only within the Religious Fundamentalist ideological surround. Within the Biblical Foundationalist ideological surround, a positive relationship with Intellect Oriented Reflection instead identified Faith Oriented Reflection as more open-minded. Complexities in these outcomes sometimes appeared in subsequent studies. The inverse connection between Faith and Intellect Oriented Reflection within the Religious Fundamentalist and their positive relationship within the Biblical Foundationalist ideological surrounds, for example, did not always reach statistical significance (e.g., Watson, Chen, Ghorbani, and Vartanian 2015; Watson, Chen, and Morris 2014, 2018; Watson, Chen, Morris, and Stephenson 2015). The overall implication, nevertheless, remained clear. Conservative Christian perspectives in the

United States did appear to have more open psychological potentials that could be obscured by ideology.

Second, even clearer evidence of ideological influences appeared with modifications of these two Religious Reflection factors for use in cultural contexts outside the United States. Faith and Intellect Oriented Reflection displayed positive rather than negative zero-order correlations when research participants were Muslims in Iran (Ghorbani, Watson, Chen, and Dover 2013), Malaysia (Tekke et al. 2015), and Pakistan (Khan, Watson, and Chen 2018). A positive relationship also appeared among Hindus in India (Kamble et al. 2014). These cross-cultural contrasts could not be explained by differences between Muslims and Hindus on the one hand and Christians on the other. Christians in Iran, unlike those in the United States, also displayed a direct rather than an inverse zero-order relationship between Faith and Intellect Oriented Reflection (Watson, Ghorbani, Vartanian, and Chen 2015). In addition, Religious Reflection factors only correlated positively in Turkish Muslims living in Germany after statistical procedures controlled for fundamentalism (S. Demmrich and H. Akce, personal communication, October 4, 2018). This Muslim result in the West, therefore, paralleled the American Christian data. In short, cross-cultural ideological influences apparently inhibited conservative religious openness in the West but encouraged it elsewhere.

Third, the ISM has argued that these cross-cultural contrasts occurred because secularism in the West has encouraged the embrace of derivative inferences that defensively close the conservatively religious mind (Watson, Chen, Morris, and Stephenson 2015). Operationalization of a Defense against Secularism (DAS) Scale made it possible to test this hypothesis. Representative of this measure were such statements as "Reason is a weapon that the culture uses to destroy faith" and "Secularist beliefs urge the use of reason and open-mindedness in political life because the real motive is to destroy our religious beliefs." DAS correlated positively with both Religious Fundamentalism and Biblical Foundationalism, but this relationship was more robust within the Religious Fundamentalist ideological surround (also see, Watson, Chen, and Morris 2018). Most importantly, however, DAS at least partially and often fully mediated linkages of conservative religiousness with intellectual closed-mindedness. DAS, for example, fully explained the negative relationship of Faith with Intellect Oriented Reflection in American Christians. Secularism as a perceived threat to faith, therefore, appears to serve as an ideological influence that defensively closes the conservatively religious Western mind. Conservative religious openness rather than closedness outside the West presumably occurs because secularism as a perceived threat is not as influential in non-Western cultural contexts.

5.2 Fundamentalism outside the West

Further evidence of ideological influences on religious openness has appeared in examinations of various indices of fundamentalism outside the West. These measures have included not only the Religious Fundamentalism Scale (Altemeyer and Hunsberger 2004), but also a version of the Post-Critical Beliefs Scale as modified for use in Iran (Duriez, Soenens, and Hutsebaut 2005), the Truth of Texts and Teaching (TTT) factor from the Religious Schema Scale (Streib, Hood, and Klein 2010), and the Intratextual Fundamentalism Scale (Williamson et al. 2010). As with Faith Oriented Reflection, data for these indices of fundamentalism outside the West confirm that conservative religiousness has potentials for more open and usually but not always healthier forms of psychological functioning.

Included in the Post-Critical Beliefs Scale are an essentially fundamentalist Transcendence and a theoretically more open-minded Symbolism factor. In an initial investigation of Iranian university students, these two factors correlated negatively; and Transcendence and Symbolism predicted stronger and weaker religious commitments, respectively (Ghorbani, Watson, Shamohammadi, and Cunningham 2009). These Iranian Muslim results, therefore, mirrored Western data in suggesting an incompatibility between faith and the presumed greater openness of Symbolism.

Other findings supported a very different conclusion. In complex results across three samples, Transcendence was largely more open and psychologically healthier than Symbolism. This outcome appeared, for example, when Transcendence predicted higher mindfulness and lower depression whereas Symbolism displayed an opposite pattern of relationships. Especially noteworthy were other analyses that used interactions between high Transcendence and low Symbolism to define a Literal Affirmation type of fundamentalist commitment (Wulff 1997). Literal Affirmation described the highest levels of psychological openness as measured by need for cognition, openness to experience, attributional complexity, and integrative self-knowledge. Hence, the fundamentalism of Transcendence (e.g., "God has been defined for once and for all and therefore is immutable"), not Symbolism (e.g., "God grows together with the history of humanity and therefore is changeable"), served as an empirical marker of Iranian Muslim psychological openness and mental health.

A later Iranian study added other constructs to the analysis of these Post Critical Beliefs (Ghorbani, Watson, Sarmast, and Chen 2018). Faith and Intellect Oriented Reflection once again correlated positively in Iran, and the appearance of this relationship in Islamic seminarians as well as in university students supplied even stronger evidence of a compatibility between Muslim faith and intellect. Most importantly, however, Transcendence correlated positively and Symbolism correlated negatively with both Faith and Intellect Oriented Reflection in both student groups. Some complexities did appear. Transcendence, for example, predicted greater rumination in university students and reduced life satisfaction in seminarians. Still, Intellect Oriented Religious Reflection data in particular supplied clear support for the conclusion that the fundamentalism of Transcendence represented a more open and Symbolism a more closed Iranian religious perspective.

Most recently, another Iranian investigation combined Post-Critical Beliefs with the Religious Fundamentalism Scale to further document the relative though not absolute mental health advantages of Muslim conservative religiousness (Ghorbani, Watson, Rabiee, and Chen 2018). Transcendence and Religious Fundamentalism correlated positively with each other and negatively with Symbolism. Other relationships confirmed Transcendence and Religious Fundamentalism as compatible and Symbolism as incompatible with Muslim attitudes and spirituality. The better mental health of Transcendence and Religious Fundamentalism appeared when one or both measures correlated positively with adaptive narcissism and self-control and negatively with maladaptive narcissism and three factors from a scale that recorded the defense mechanism of splitting. The poorer mental health of Symbolism seemed obvious in negative correlations with self-control, integrative self-knowledge, and mindfulness and in positive linkages with maladjusted narcissism and all three splitting measures. Complexities did appear, however, when Transcendence and Religious Fundamentalism correlated positively with one or both measures of a dependency that had problematic psychological implications. Still, the overall suggestion of these data was clear. Conservative Iranian Muslim perspectives, and not Symbolism, pointed toward the more psychologically adaptive social rationality.

The potential openness of conservative religiousness has also appeared in findings for TTT. The fundamentalism of this measure contrasts with a Xenosophia factor from the same Religious Schema Scale. Xenosophia records beliefs that a wisdom (*sophia*) can be discovered within the perspectives of outsiders (*xeno*) and appears in such claims as, "The truth I see in other world views leads me to re-examine my current views." The fundamentalism of TTT appears in such assertions as, "What the texts and stories of my religion tell me is absolutely true and must not be changed." A negative correlation with Xenosophia is one among many findings that identify TTT as a more closed-minded perspective in the West.

Outside the West, however, TTT has correlated positively rather than negatively with Xenosophia. This relationship appeared with Muslims from Iran

(Ghorbani, Watson, Amirbeigi, and Chen 2016; Ghorbani, Watson, Chen, and Dover 2013), Malaysia (Tekke et al. 2015), and Pakistan (Khan, Watson, and Chen 2017); Hindus from India (Kamble et al. 2014); and Christians from Iran (Watson, Ghorbani, Vartanian, and Chen 2015). In the one study that added the Religious Reflection Scale to the analysis, TTT and Xenosophia also correlated positively with both Faith and Intellect Orientated Reflection in Indian Hindus (Kamble et al. 2014). Data for TTT, therefore, once again demonstrated that potentials for conservative religious openness exist in non-Western, less secularized cultural contexts.

A later study of Hindus in India not only replicated the positive TTT linkage with Xenosophia but also demonstrated that the Religious Fundamentalism and Intratextual Fundamentalism scales had complex potentials for openness as well (Kamble et al. 2018). Unlike TTT, these two other scales included reverse scored expressions of fundamentalism that reduced their internal reliabilities to unacceptably low levels. Elimination of those items produced psychometrically sounder instruments that correlated positively with the open-mindedness of Xenosophia. The items removed from Intratextual Fundamentalism correlated positively with TTT whereas removed Religious Fundamentalism items correlated negatively. These psychometric complexities suggested that Western operationalizations of fundamentalism lacked ideological coherence when used with Indian Hindus. With a previous Iranian Muslim sample, the Fundamentalism Scale was internally reliable (Ghorbani, Watson, Rabiee, and Chen 2018); so, this problem does not generalize across all non-Western contexts. Still, positive linkages of Xenosophia with TTT in India and with the modified Intratextual Fundamentalism and Religious Fundamentalism measures once again demonstrated that conservative religiousness has potentials for openness outside the West.

5.3   *Christian Religious Xenophilia*
One final support for the Religious Openness Hypothesis has appeared in a recent reexamination of well-established findings that fundamentalism predicts xenophobia in the West. This fear (*phobia*) of outsiders (*xeno*) becomes obvious, for example, when the Religious Fundamentalism Scale correlates positively with various indices of prejudice (e.g., Altemeyer and Hunsberger 1992, 2004; Hunsberger 1996). For the ISM, however, objectivity requires a holistic conceptualization of religious traditions as complex, hierarchically organized social rationalities. That xenophobia can be located within the derivative inferences of such hierarchies does not mean that other, very different potentials cannot be discovered as well. Derivative inferences associated with a love (*philia*) of outsiders (*xeno*) may also exist. The operationalization of a

Religious Xenophilia Scale confirmed this possibility (Watson, Reagan, Chen, and Morris, forthcoming).

A perhaps most obvious reason for expecting to discover Christian xenophilia as a derivative inference may appear in the Christian echo (Mark 12:31) of the Jewish belief that one should love of one's neighbor (Leviticus 19:18). The suggestion of Mark 12:30 is that this love rests upon a prior love of God. The parable of the Good Samaritan then deepens the analysis by implying that a neighbor is whoever happens to be nearby (Luke 10:23–37). A summary expression of this social rationality may appear, for example, in 1 John 4:7–8: "Beloved, let us love one another, for love is from God, and whoever loves has been born of God and knows God. Anyone who does not love does not know God, because God is love." In other words, God as love is the ultimate standard, and love of neighbor is the derivative inference.

Placher (1994) notes the prominence of xenophilia in early Christian thought when he points out, "The New Testament word for 'hospitality,' *philoxenia*, means 'love of strangers'; it is the opposite of xenophobia, the fear of those whom one does not know" (p. 153). He further clarifies this idea by quoting Justin Martyr, a Christian apologist of the Second Century, who said, "There is not ... one single race of [people]—whether barbarians, Greeks, or persons called by any other name, nomads, or vagabonds, or herdsmen dwelling in tents—among whom prayers and thanksgiving are not offered to the Father and Creator of the universe in the name of the Crucified Jesus" (Justin Martyr as quoted in Placher, p. 154). Placher concludes that "New Testament texts find a variety of ways to challenge the model of a community of insiders who exclude" (p. 153). Inclusion not exclusion should define Christian community. Xenophilia and not just xenophobia should appear as a derivative inference within Christian social rationalities.

Empirical confirmation of this suggestion occurred in a study that used an American Christian sample to create a Religious Xenophilia Scale that included Xenophilic Love and Xenophilic Grace factors. Two kinds of statements reflected Xenophilic Love. Some expressed love of others as a general principle (e.g., "My religious beliefs motivate me to love all people" and "All people are equally deserving of God's love, regardless of who they are"). Others spelled out more particularly the "outsiders" who should be loved including other races, sinners, people with emotional problems, those with HIV, and individuals representing different educational levels, occupations, political beliefs, countries, and religions. Six *reverse* scored statements defined Xenophilic Grace. Illustrative items said, "My religious traditions make it clear that love should only be shown to those who are moral," "People who sin constantly are not worthy of love," and "To be faithful to my religion,

I should reject people whose political beliefs differ from mine." Reversed scoring meant that these items expressed a rejection of morality and religiously based condemnations of outsiders and thus revealed an extension of grace to them.

In zero-order relationships, Xenophilic Love and Grace correlated positively with each other and displayed clear linkages with such measures of conservative religiosity as Religious Fundamentalism, Biblical Foundationalism, and TTT. Both also correlated negatively with a social dominance orientation that predicts xenophobia (Pratto, Sidanius, Stallworth, and Malle 1994) and with the exploitative impulsiveness of psychopathy (Jonason and Webster 2010). Also noteworthy were positive correlations of Xenophilic Love and with all four factors of the Extrinsic Cultural Religious Orientation Scale (Watson, Chen, and Ghorbani 2014). This measure records motivations to use religion to promote the common good and includes a Peace and Justice factor that says, for example, "My motivation for being religious is a desire to develop a human society that is peaceful, just, and happy." Positive Xenophilic Love relationships with Peace and Justice seemed especially useful in documenting conservative Christian potentials for social openness.

Statistical controls for ideology documented the psychosocially problematic implications of Religious Fundamentalism. In partial correlations controlling for Biblical Foundationalism, Religious Fundamentalism correlated *negatively* with Xenophilic Love and non-significantly with Xenophilic Grace. A positive partial correlation with TTT was just one finding that identified Religious Fundamentalism as a valid index of conservative Christian commitments. Inverse associations with Xenosophia and with Peace and Justice along with a direct linkage with the social dominance orientation confirmed Religious Fundamentalism as psychologically more closed.

In contrast, partial correlations controlling for Religious Fundamentalism uncovered *direct* relationships of Biblical Foundationalism with both Xenophilic Love and Xenophilic Grace. A direct relationship with TTT in these procedures was among the findings that also confirmed Biblical Foundationalism as a conservative Christian perspective. The greater openness and psychological adjustment of Biblical Foundationalism appeared as well in partial correlations that were positive with Xenosophia and with Peace and Justice and negative with social dominance orientation and psychopathy.

The hypothesis of this study had been that Religious Xenophilia would be more closed within a Religious Fundamentalist and more open within a Biblical Foundationalist ideological surround. This result did not appear because Religious Xenophilia factors turned out to reflect a conservative religiosity that predicted greater openness and psychological adjustment within both ideological surrounds. Xenophilic Love, for example, correlated positively across both ideological surrounds with TTT, Xenosophia, and Peace and Justice and negatively with social dominance orientation and psychopathy. Xenophilic Grace also predicted higher TTT scores and lower levels of social dominance orientation and psychopathy.

The ISM operationalization of Christian traditions dealing with xenophilia combined with statistical controls for ideology pointed toward three most important points relative to the Religious Openness Hypothesis. First, and most obviously, conservative Christian commitments have potentials not only for fear of the stranger, but also for love of the stranger. Such a demonstration in no way means that the problematic implications of Christian xenophobia should be ignored. The suggestion instead is that a more comprehensive and thus 'objective' analysis of these issues means that Christian social rationalities should not be stereotyped and scapegoated in terms of an exclusive focus on their negative potentials. An empirically 'truthful' study of relationships between psychology and religion should include an examination of the prosocial possibilities that may also operate within Christian and other religious traditions.

Second, Xenophilic Love data were especially noteworthy. In partial correlations controlling for Religious Fundamentalism, Biblical Foundationalism correlated *positively* with Xenophilic Love, and within this Biblical Foundationalist ideological surround, Xenophilic Love also predicted the fundamentalism of TTT, greater social openness, and better psychological adjustment. These findings pointed toward conservative integrity in an embrace of Christian love and openness. In contrast, Religious Fundamentalism after controlling for Biblical Foundationalism correlated *negatively* with Xenophilic Love, but *surprisingly*, Xenophilic Love within this Religious Fundamentalist ideological surround still predicted the fundamentalism of TTT, greater social openness, and better psychological adjustment. These data pointed instead toward a lack of integrity between conservative Christian commitments and the conservative Christian dynamics of xenophilia. Once again, an ideological splitting associated with fundamentalism seemed to be influential within conservative religious perspectives in the West.

A third and final point leads to more complex issues. A basic skepticism about the Religious Openness Hypothesis might begin with the complaint that it is simply too naïve because it ignores recent history. Recent history clearly documents the dangerous connections that can exist between closed-minded conservative religiousness and violence. Any focus on religious xenophilia would, therefore, obscure dangerous potentials that should instead be the foreground concern.

An ISM response to this skepticism would emphasize three points of clarification and extension associated with previously mentioned issues. A first point of clarification would begin with the social scientific understanding that correlation cannot prove causation. Just because conservative religiosity and violence can go together does not mean that the former is a simple cause that can explain the latter as a simple effect. Indeed, a careful review of the historical record can suggest that political factors caused violence in religion as much as or more than religious factors causing violence in political life. Evidence supporting this conclusion appears in analyses the Thirty Years' War in the West (Cavanaugh 2009), the Muslim response to British colonialism on the Indian subcontinent (Jalal 2008), and contemporary expressions of jihadism as holy war (Mekhennet 2017).

A second clarification returns to studies using the Defense against Secularism Scale with American Christians (Watson, Chen, and Morris 2018; Watson, Chen, Morris, and Stephenson 2015). These data and the broader literature supporting the Religious Openness Hypothesis combine to suggest that conservative religious potentials for openness may become closed through the mediation political influences. Conservative Christian closed-mindedness may, therefore, appear as a correlation explained at least to some important degree by political factors as a cause that produce transformations in religious beliefs as an effect.

A third and final clarification may appear in an extension of these points to the work of Sen, Wagner, and Howarth (2014), who used qualitative research methods to analyze why conflicts between Hindus and Muslim seem to threaten democracy in India. One of their Hindu research participants argued, "Politicians create the problems and they will never let the issue die because communal tensions serve their interests" (Sen et al., p. 9). A roughly parallel claim came from a Muslim who observed, "Generally common Hindus are good and they do not want trouble of any sort but it is the communal [political] parties in India who instigate them to create a communal atmosphere" (Sen et al., p. 10). Another Muslim offered a summarizing understanding of how "this ideology [of xenophobia] emerged" by saying, "There is a conflict of powerful and powerless and this is a breeding ground for [a] few people, who have hardly anything to do with spirituality but are interested only in their political and economic interests." He then adds, "This is a major role that the world community has to do. It is to counter this myth and show that it is purely political interest, which drives terrorism and terrorism has nothing to do with religion" (Sen et al., p. 26). Relative to the ISM, this last point is profoundly important. If political factors are a cause of religious violence as an effect, then theist and indeed many other social rationalities have a social scientific obligation to empirically document that influence.

A contrast between one item from the Religious Fundamentalism Scale and a statement made by one of the Sen et al. (2014) Muslim research participants may usefully summarize how cultural context may help close the conservatively religious mind (Kamble et al. 2018). The relevant Religious Fundamentalism item says, "The basic cause of evil in this world is Satan, who is still constantly and ferociously fighting against God." The existence of Satan seems to make the situation clear in the West. A culture war must be fought against this ferocious and evil opponent of God. The Muslim research participant observed, instead, "Satan is most happy when people fight among themselves" (Sen et al., p. 51). Outside the more secular West, it may be more possible to see the violence of politics and xenophobia as a war of Satan against God. Within these non-Western ideological surrounds, support of God against Satan would presumably require a refusal to participate in xenophobic wars.

5.4 Methodological Theism as Necessary for 'Objectivity'

Theist methodological dialogism supplements other aspects of the ISM to argue that objectivity in the study of psychology and religion requires empirically guided dialogues among multiple theisms and of these theisms with atheisms. The incommensurability of these social rationalities will mean that any triumphalist explanatory framework based upon one specific ultimate standard could be epistemologically useful but will also be constrained by its own normative and sociological limitations. In the absence of a master ultimate standard for making judgements across ideological surrounds, such monological triumphalisms cannot be dismissed as unquestionably irrational. Indeed, monological triumphalisms are an undeniable and influential empirical reality, and 'objectivity' requires a model of psychology and religion that makes a place for them. The ISM does this by emphasizing that the monological triumphalisms of both psychology and theisms may have contributions to make.

At the same time, however, monological triumphalisms are vulnerable to a ghettoization that prevents them from seeing the complexities of social rationalities across ideological surrounds. A social rationality matures as its thought and practice are brought into conformity with the perceived demands of its ultimate standard. As Nietzsche (1887/1967) suggests, standards of science and religion both include 'truth' as an essential derivative inference. A ghettoized perspective may refuse to see how other ideological surrounds live meaningfully according to the understandings they have of their own 'truth' and may consequently offer incomplete or mistaken interpretations of those outside social rationalities. A mismatch could then appear between the assertions of a ghettoized perspective and the reliable and valid observations that can be made across ideological surrounds. Correspondence between assertions and empirical observations would help define 'truth.' A triumphalism taken to an extreme would, therefore, violate its own commitment to 'truth' and would make it susceptible to authoritarianism.

Dialogue is the proposed ISM solution for the problems of incommensurability and ghettoization. Theist social scientists should operationalize their traditions and document the meaningfulness of religious rationalities. The normative assumptions of methodological and metaphysical atheists and of religious synthesizers and anti-psychological theists should then be brought into empirically guided dialogues with methodological theism in an attempt to encourage the maturation of theist social rationalities. Such research programs would be essential in advancing the rationality and sociological viability of religious traditions across generations.

In the opposite direction, atheist social scientists should also respond to the work of methodological and metaphysical theists. In doing so, they of course will not embrace theist ultimate standards. Instead, their responses to dialogical observations about theism should allow them to adjust their derivative inferences about religion relative to their own ultimate standards. Correspondence between assertions and observations could grow, and atheist social rationalities could mature through attention to the work of methodological theists.

Atheist resistances to dialogue might reflect a reluctance to even admit the problems of incommensurable rationality and ideology. To do so might seem to threaten social scientific beliefs in 'truth' and 'objectivity' as expressed, for example, in methodological commitments to reliability and validity. Theist methodological dialogism, nevertheless, offers reliable and valid demonstrations that ideology impacts both psychology and religion. This is clear in the psychometric deconstructions of psychometrics and in the expansion of dialogue to religions and cultures outside the West. Such data document ideology as a 'truth' in the study of psychology and religion, and this 'truth' in no way threatens 'objectivity.'

Perhaps most generally, the ISM seeks to open up understandings of psychology and religion in a way that points toward an 'objectivity' that does not facilely dismiss social rationalities as benighted or sinful forms of thought and practice that must be explained away. Triumphalists can and will work toward such goals. Alternatively, followers of outside ideological surrounds can be seen as dialogical partners who can cooperate in the 'truthful' maturation of social rationalities across both religious and psychological perspectives. Dialogism, therefore, has a potential to socially construct greater rationality in public space. For at least some, greater rationality in public space would be an empirically obvious need.

6   Dialogue and Trans-rationality

At perhaps the most abstract level, the ISM argues that reason in the social sciences needs to be submitted to the further analysis of reason. Dominant perspectives in contemporary psychology have at least implicit foundations in Enlightenment beliefs that reason is the monological product of an individual (Sampson 1993). Appropriately disciplined by method, such individuals supposedly possess clear and distinct ideas about what is rational and what is irrational. The overall presumption is that "the mind of man is intendedly rational and scientific ... the dictates of reason are equally binding for all regardless of time, place, culture, race, personal desire, or individual endowment ... in reason can be found a universally applicable standard for judging validity and worth" (Shweder as quoted by Sampson, p. 78). Freud (1927/1961a) illustrates this perspective when he argues that "nothing can withstand reason and experience" as expressed in science (Freud, p. 54). The conclusion seems clear. Science supplies humanity with monologues of a master rationality, "a universally applicable standard for judging validity and worth."

Descartes' *cogito*, his "I think; therefore, I am," might be read as an epistemological manifesto for Enlightenment monological triumphalism. "What Descartes and his successors said, in effect, was that there are an awful lot of meanings and opinions about, that they cannot all be right, and that we'd better find, and justify, a yardstick which will sort out the sheep from the goats" (Gellner 1992, p. 38). Those successors eventually expressed themselves in agnostic and then atheist ideological surrounds that assumed, "Ideally, one needs clear principles, like those of the scientific method, which can divide the sheep from the goats among the beliefs that try to nestle in our minds" (Taylor 1989, p. 405). In these Enlightenment transformations of Matthew 25:32, Nature as revealed in the reason and experience of science eventually replaces God as the ultimate standard in the monologues of a master rationality that can shepherd rational sheep through social life after the irrational goats have been expelled from the flock.

Relationships between psychology and religion present a formidable challenge to this nonreligious monologism. The atheism of advanced Enlightenment thought presumes that beliefs in 'God' can be explained away by translating them fully into inferences derived from Nature as the ultimate standard. In other words, 'God' can be falsified scientifically. The problem of incommensurability will mean, however, that belief in the falsification of God will make sense, but *only* within specific ideological surrounds. Social rationalities operate as systematic patterns of thought and practice that are brought under the perceived normative demands of different ultimate standards. For theists, God will be the ultimate standard, and no higher ultimate standard will be available for falsifying it. Only a noncontroversial master rationality can falsify psychological or religious rationalities, but incommensurability will mean that no such rationality will be logically available. Monological social rationalities in science and in religion too, therefore, need to be supplemented by something else.

6.1 *"I dialogue; therefore, I am"*

Descartes can perhaps be read as an apologist for scientific monological rationality, but that was not his obvious intent. This is a complicated story, but an indication of his very different approach appears in the fact that his *cogito* was not the clear and distinct idea of an isolated individual. Descartes instead took this notion from Saint Augustine and extended it in what eventually proved to be modernist directions (Taylor 1989). This and numerous other aspects of his thought make it clear Descartes' arguments emerged out of his dialogues with Catholic tradition (Taylor 1989; Gaukroger 1995; MacIntyre 2009).

Descartes' work, therefore, points toward the potentials of dialogical social rationalities. Within the ISM, dialogism is the 'something else' that should supplement the monologisms that exist in relationships between psychology and religion. Rather than Descartes' *cogito*, the operating principle should be, "I dialogue; therefore, I am." Dialogical rationalities are not univocal and turn out instead to be at least three distinct rationalities (Watson 2014).

6.2 *Private Rationality: "I reflect; therefore, I am"*

Dialogical rationalities are private rationalities. Privacy and dialogue may seem like polar opposites, but Dialogical Self Theory (DST) describes how intricate relationships necessarily exist between the two (Hermans and Kempen 1993). In line with William James, DST assumes that the self operates as a composite involving an 'I' in combination with a 'me.' The 'me' involves aspects of the self that can be known. The 'I' is the psychological process that does the knowing. DST then follows Mikhail Bakhtin in rejecting a Cartesian reification of the 'I' as an autonomous source of rationality. Instead of being an independent agency of clear and distinct ideas, the 'I' turns out to be a position elicited within consciousness by relationships with actual or imagined others. This 'I-position' then accounts for the 'me' as it appears in dialogical interactions with others. Private rationality, therefore, appears an always on-going social construction of dialogues.

In the absence of additional assumptions, DST would depict the self as a centrifugal disintegration of disconnected I-position compounds reflecting diverse dialogical contexts. A self, nevertheless, has an identity that includes a sense of "continuity, distinctness, and volition" (Hermans and Kempen 1993, p. 44). Countervailing centripetal processes, therefore, emerge as a meta-perspectival I-position that "has the capacity to juxtapose and interrelate the other positions that neither apart nor in their incidental relationships can achieve any synthesis of the self as a whole" (Hermans and Kempen, p. 92). This meta-I then "shows considerable differences between people and within one and the same person over time" (p. 101). This vision of the self has three most noteworthy implications for the ISM.

First, the dialogical private self can be interpreted as a rationality that operates according to the principle, "I reflect; therefore, I am." This would not be a modernist Cartesian self that somehow presupposed it could independently generate its own light for discovering clear and distinct ideas. Light instead would arise from relationships that brought dialogical insight to bear on the hierarchically organized structures of the me within the self. Descartes' dialogues with Saint Augustine and Catholic traditions would illustrate reflected light.

This suggestion in no way challenges notions of personal creativity and genius because the light of a meta-I could reflect in 'inventive' and 'brilliant' new directions. Methods of skepticism, reductionism, induction, and comprehensive rational analysis, for instance, might be seen as historically ingenious within Cartesian private rationality and within modernist rationality more generally. The presumption, however, would be that no neutral, dialogue-free cultural space could be found for developing a Cartesian or any other private rationality. All private rationalities operate within dialogical and thus ideological social surrounds. This realization would define the foundations of what might be called the Dialogical Enlightenment.

Second, within private rationality, perspectives of a meta-I would describe a self that essentially served as a somewhat nonempirical ultimate standard that would have its own normative and sociological implications. That ultimate standard, like all others, should not be hypostatized because it can change within a person across time, as DST makes clear. Private rationalities can, of course, mature in two ways. The thought and practice of the private self can be brought into better conformity with the perceived demands of the self. Alternatively, the application of inferences derived from meta-I might reveal a need for modifications in visions of the self and/or for the development of more effective derivative inferences. Of course, private rationalities could also fail to mature through processes of ghettoization that walled out dialogues with outside voices that seemed to be threatening, sinful, or wholly irrational. In processes of maturation, however, new dialogues with those outside voices should receive open consideration. Results of those dialogues, however, would necessarily require adjudication by the meta-I. Even rejected dialogical discernments could be integrated as rationally unacceptable into the consequently more insightful and expansive hierarchical structures of the self.

Third, analysis of private rationalities can help clarify relationships between psychology and religion. In a first example of this possibility, the idea that self-actualization can be expressed in Christian language would reflect the dynamics of private rationality. Through prayer, Bible study, interactions with other believers, and the reading of books about Christianity, a Christian could receive a socially constructed I-position that created dialogues between the 'me' and Christ. Those dialogues would then encourage Christian self-actualization. Parallel statements could apply to the private rationalities of other religious traditions. In addition, the problematic impacts of Defense against Secularism and the fundamentalist rejection of Xenophilic Love point toward the ideological splitting of ghettoization within the private rationality of the Western Christian self. Ghettoization and ideological splitting could appear in other religious traditions as well. Finally, role-taking theory assumes that religious believers can discover within religious texts a role that they can take in their relationship with God and their tradition (Van der Lans 1987). Role-taking would reflect processes of private rationality in which text-produced I-positions brought the 'me' of believers into dialogue with God.

6.3 Communal Rationality: "I agree; therefore, I am"

Dialogical rationalities are also communal rationalities in which the operating principle is, "I agree; therefore, I am." Communal rationalities organize themselves around shared commitments to what meta-I perspectives across individuals perceive to be the same ultimate standard. That ultimate standard could be God, Nature, or Power, or more likely one or another more specific expression of each. Christian, Hindu, Muslim, and other religions, for instance, organize themselves around different tradition-specific visions of God. Similarly, psychoanalysis, radical behaviorism, cognitivism, and other schools of thought organize themselves around different understandings of Nature within contemporary psychology. Shared commitments to the same somewhat nonempirical ultimate standard would have normative and sociological implications for the communal rationalities of the social sciences as well as of religion.

Communal rationalities would not be without disagreements. Those disagreements, however, would operate at the level of derivative inferences, not at the level of ultimate standards. In Christianity, for instance, such differences can appear across denominations, across congregations within a denomination, and across individuals within a single congregation. Contrasts between

Religious Fundamentalism and Biblical Foundationalism would be an example. Discord about derivative inferences would ideally serve as a dialogical stimulus for the maturation of religious traditions. That maturation would require more expansive visions of the ultimate standard and/or the development of more insightful derivative inferences. Movements toward ghettoization could instead occur when visions of the ultimate standard eventually no longer seemed to be the same. Schismatic separations would result when a previously united community could no longer be guided by the assertion, "I agree; therefore, I am." With such outcomes, tendencies toward atomization, fragmentation, and polarization would be enhanced within the wider culture.

Relative to the ISM, this perspective on communal rationalities points toward at least two important issues. First, private and communal rationalities are not independent but rather operate in dynamic interaction. Role-taking theory supplies an easy example. The dialogues and texts associated with a community will suggest a range of available roles available for those who find themselves in agreement about what should be their ultimate standard. Members of that community will then integrate one or more of those roles within the meta-I of their private rationality. Communities will then supply a 'stage' upon which the 'scripts' of those roles can be performed. 'Performances' will then strengthen the role and the ultimate standard within the 'performer,' which in turn will strengthen the community as a place to 'stage' its derivative inferences. Private identity formation would promote community maturation and vice versa.

Second, reemphasis should be placed on the notion that social sciences, like religions, are communities with their own somewhat nonempirical ultimate standards of rationality. Descartes (1637/1968), for example, argued for a wider dissemination of the experimental results recommended by his method "so that the last beginning where their predecessors had left off, and thereby linking the lives and the labors of many, we might all together go much further than each man could individually" (p. 79). In other words, the 'I' of the *cogito* was not presumed to be an individualist working in isolation on clear and distinct ideas but rather a community of 'I's' with their lives linked together.

With absolutely no disrespect intended, therefore, social sciences and different perspectives within a single social science might be conceptualized as 'denominations' committed to Nature. Graduate schools would serve as 'monasteries' where future 'priests' learn acceptable 'doctrine.' After graduation, those 'priests' would stage their performances in, for example, classrooms, laboratories, professional meetings, journal articles, and peer-reviews. Successful performances could then lead to opportunities for advancement toward the roles of "bishop," "archbishop," "cardinal," and "pope." Freud, for example, was a 'pope' of the psychoanalytic vision of Nature. Nietzsche, incidentally, was a "pope" of Power who favored the traditions of the Roman Empire over those of Israel.

In short, the argument of the ISM is that in the absence of an indisputable master rationality, escape from tradition is impossible. Social sciences are no different from religions in being somewhat nonempirical, normative, and sociological, and both share nonnegotiable derivative inferences like 'truth' and "objectivity." The assumption could not be, therefore, that social sciences are somehow truthful and objective whereas religions are not. Both pursue truthfulness and objectivity within the surround of their own ideological assumptions. Both can mature. Both can stagnate through ghettoization. More generally, 'truth' and 'objectivity' in the empirical study of psychology and religion require analyses of these incommensurable rationalities and of the dialogues that can exist between them.

6.4   Public Rationality: "I disagree; therefore, I am"

Rationalities within public space follow the principle, "I disagree; therefore, I am." Again, persons and communities can argue in public space over ultimate standards in a manner that implies that one rationality can defeat another through logic alone. In this confusion of a communal with a public rationality, the problem of incommensurability makes such presumptions wholly suspect. Logical defeat of one ideology by another requires appeal to a shared higher standard for adjudicating differences. Ideologies, however, are committed to somewhat nonempirical ultimate standards, and any attempt to hold an ultimate standard accountable to some higher standard of adjudication would make it non-ultimate. Non-ultimate, ultimate standards are a logical contradiction and an impossibility. Public space consequently becomes vulnerable to arguments that are interminable and unproductive.

Disagreements in public space can also occur at the level of derivative inferences. Examples in one society or another would include derivative inferences about wearing a hijab in certain public spaces, abortion, gay rights, prayer in school, public displays of religious symbols, and many more. Despite such disagreements, the ISM emphasizes that derivative inferences can also present a critical opportunity for socially constructing agreement in public space. Across public and communal rationalities, that effort would begin with an identification of derivate inferences that could serve as provisional standards of dialogical adjudication. For the ISM, those provisional standards necessarily include 'truth' and 'objectivity,' both of which rest upon a correspondence between assertions and observations. Incommensurability will mean that this correspondence cannot be established through the use of rational insight alone.

Adjudications should be mediated instead through empirical observations that comply with social scientific derivative inferences associated with reliability and validity. This interpretation of public space points toward at least six important implications for the ISM.

First, commitments to 'truth' and 'objectivity' will seem passé at best or reactionary at worst within at least some ideological surrounds. The ISM remains committed to dialogue; so, if better provisional standards of adjudication can be agreed upon, then so be it. Still, the nagging question will remain, "Who would want to enter into dialogue with any individuals or communities who failed hold to themselves accountable to some standards of truth and objectivity?" Of course, public definitions of 'truth' and 'objectivity' would likely require dialogical negotiation, but some mutually agreed upon definition would seem to be essential.

Second, rejections of 'truth' and 'objectivity' as dialogical standards might reflect fears that these derivative inferences could be used for authoritarian domination. The worry here might be that advocates of the 'truth' of one ultimate standard would attempt to use it to defeat the 'falsehoods' of all other ultimate standards. 'Truth' would here become a weapon rather than a dialogical tool. The ISM finds this fear to be unfounded. In a world of incommensurable social rationalities, dialogues in public space cannot bring disagreements to a conclusion. Somewhat nonempirical ultimate standards cannot be dismissed logically or falsified empirically. Any tendency toward authoritarian domination would presumably reflect a use of power, not a commitment to truth and objectivity. Instead of authoritarianism, truth and objectivity will have a potential to advance disagreements in more authoritative directions. Again, dialogical standards of adjudication can make disagreements in public space interminable but more productive.

Third, boundaries between public and communal space are fluid. Disagreements in public space, for example, might threaten society with a cultural disintegration characterized by a metaphorical or an increasingly literal war of all against all (Girard 1978). Identification of an enemy to blame for all this chaos presents society with a scapegoat against which those disagreements can be projected through ostracism or violence. Through this process of scapegoating, unity replaces disunity as public space attempts to use violence to transform itself into communal space. Authoritarian, but not authoritative, regimes of understanding would presumably find scapegoating to be especially useful for achieving social solidarity. Again, the ISM rejects authoritarianism and also scapegoating (Watson 1998, 2004).

Fourth, the ISM description of public space may suggest a capitulation to relativism, but this is absolutely not the case. Relativism in public space is an empirical reality; so, objectivity requires a rational and empirical appreciation of its existence. On the other hand, relativism as interpreted by the ISM cannot become an ultimate standard and cannot make normative demands. How can the nonexistence of ultimate standards become an ultimate standard without becoming an ultimate standard that logically contradicts relativism? In short, the ISM admits relativism as an empirical reality but then seeks the development of social scientific perspectives that work against any attempts to make its implications normative.

Fifth, dialogue based upon shared derivative inferences presents the social sciences with an opportunity to contribute to the essential task of constructing cooperation in public space. The perhaps mistaken diagnosis of the ISM is that contemporary circumstances strengthen private and certain communal rationalities at the expense of public rationality. Public rationalities must cope with the narcissism of selves and with the narcissism of triumphalist communities, with all this tending toward atomization, fragmentation, and polarization. Public life gets trapped in 'cyclical history' in which centripetal domination by one or another social rationality sets the stage for centrifugal resistances by the other, dominated social rationalities. Abrasive disintegrations of centripetal processes then occur as a centrifugal response. Centrifugal disintegration then encourages a chaos that justifies a return to one or another centripetal domination as a way to reestablish order in a never-ending cycle (see e.g., Fukuyama 2006). The ISM assumes that the way out of cyclical history is 'linear' history in which social rationalities find opportunities to pursue their own eschatological maturation. Maturations would occur in communal space, but dialogue in public space could be useful as well. Ultimately, the broader ideological maturation of linear histories could encourage a more socially beneficial dialectical unfolding of centripetal and centrifugal forces in public social life.

Finally, the ISM description of public space suggests a continuum of roles for the social sciences. At one extreme, a research program might pursue triumphalist objectives in public space based upon a confidence that all other social rationalities are actually irrationalities that can and should be colonized. Freud (1927/1961) would be an obvious example. At the opposite extreme, a research program might attempt to pursue only a methodological dialogism. The presumption might be that an unmitigated dialogism would offer 'neutrality' as an escape from ideology. The ISM argues, however, that ideology cannot be escaped. All dialogisms will have their own ultimate standards which in turn will have their own normative and sociological implications. Between these extremes, the ISM argues for social scientific commitments to one or another home ideological surround supplemented by methodological dialogism. The ISM rests upon a metaphysical theism combined with a theist methodological dialogism. A different research program might combine a metaphysical atheism with an atheist methodological dialogism.

6.5 *Secularization and Trans-rationality*

For research programs dedicated to methodological atheism, metaphysical atheism is a not infrequent ideological accompaniment. Secularization, defined as the inexorable movement of individuals and societies away from theist social rationalities toward the reason and experience of science, is an at least implicit derivative inference of these metaphysical atheists. Freud (1927/1961a) again supplies the obvious example. The derivative inference of secularization presupposes that interactions between social rationalities are a zero-sum game. One social rationality becomes stronger as others necessarily becomes weaker. One social rationality must win. All others must eventually lose.

The ISM functions with very different derivative inferences. Rather than secularization, the ISM argues that social rationalities are better described by the dynamics of trans-rationality. Incommensurability and the somewhat nonempirical ultimate standards of ideologies will mean that as one social rationality becomes stronger, others will not necessarily become weaker. Secularization is naïve in its belief that there is and can be a master rationality. Rationalities are much more complex and operate at private, communal, and public levels of dialogue. Secularization mistakes the specifically communal rationality of scientific communities as the master rationality. Other communal rationalities have at least the same theoretical potential to mature as scientific rationalities. The ISM operationalization of traditions and the psychometric deconstruction of psychometrics represent attempts to document that potential. Dialogues between theist and atheist social rationalities can benefit both. Dialogues formally held accountable to standards of reliability and validity can move social rationalities toward win-win relationships.

Rejections of the idea that only win–lose relationships can exist between social rationalities will also mean that lose–lose interactions can occur as well. Indeed, the ISM diagnoses a collapse of dialogue in public space as a product of cultural forces that encourage lose–lose interactions. Triumphalisms of religion and science weaken provisional standards of dialogue in public space and encourage atomization, ghettoization, and polarization. All this moves social life toward a cyclical history in which one or another form of centripetal domination triggers centrifugal resistances in never-ending and destructive oscillations of history.

The ISM advocacy of trans-rationality in no way means that it presumes that social rationalities can never lose completely and disappear. Processes of extinction occur through ghettoization. Ghettoization can be a literal consequence of geographic isolation. A so-called primitive social rationality that comes into first contact with modernization may find itself at an overwhelming competitive disadvantage. The rationalities of modernity will display a far superior correspondence between assertions and publicly available observations. Across a fairly short number of generations, such a primitive rationality may disappear.

More importantly, however, ghettoization within a culture can also lead to the slower disappearance of a social rationality. The ISM is ideologically committed to metaphysical theism; so, its principal concern is with the ghettoization of specifically Christian and more generally religious social rationalities. As interpreted by the ISM, triumphalist religious ideological surrounds display a lack of faith that the reason and experience of science can operate as a derivative inference within theist social rationalities. This lack of faith will mean that mismatches between assertions and publicly available observations will move religious rationalities toward authoritarianism and away from authoritativeness. This might work across a shorter number of generations, but the strategy seems doomed to failure across longer time spans as increasingly large and diverse populations of naïve observers arrive on this pluralistic planet. Empirical warrant for this conclusion seems readily available in the historical record at least from the time of William of Ockham. Relative to this scenario, secularization might eventually become triumphant, not because of its superiority but rather because of the progressively inferior maturation of religious social rationalities (see e.g., Brauer 2018).

At least three clarifications seem important about this interpretation of ghettoization. First, predictions of the future are notoriously unreliable. Other scenarios might make more sense. Some may worry, for example, that one or another religious triumphalism could become a centripetal hegemony. At least some religious social rationalities would stand in opposition to any and all such hegemonic dominations. Religious centripetal hegemonies would also trigger centrifugal resistances outside religious ideological surrounds and thereby strengthen cyclical history. Actions that strengthen cyclical history would betray the eschatological aspirations of even triumphalist religious rationalities. Second, the ISM attempts to demonstrate empirically that ghettoization is not inevitable. Religious rationalities can and should mature through dialogue. Critical in the longer-term nurturance of religious rationalities will be the recruitment of talent that can then recruit and train the next generations of talent in a linear history of maturation (e.g., Johnson 2007). Failures of religious ideological surrounds to ensure this process would encourage their authoritarianism and their entrapment within secularization and cyclical history. Third, atheist ideological surrounds will also have potentials for ghettoization. This could eventuate in very different hegemonies that at least some ideological surrounds would believe can and should be resisted as well (Hart 2009).

Finally, secularization and trans-rationalities are derivative inferences reflecting different ultimate standards. As derivative inferences of incommensurable social rationalities, secularization and trans-rationality cannot be dismissed through logic alone or through empirical falsification. Efforts to do so could prove to be interminable and unproductive. The ISM would argue instead that the appropriate response to this problem would be to bring secularization and trans-rationality into dialogues that could become interminable and more productive. Derivative inferences about secularization and trans-rationality can and should be brought into win-win relationships.

6.6 *In Conclusion, ISM Inconclusion*

Incommensurability may seem to dictate relativism. The ISM admits relativism as an empirical, but not as a normative reality. A 'truthful' and 'objective' social science will construct models that describe and analyze the somewhat nonempirical ultimate standards that define social life. The relativism of social life is not a relativism of relativisms, but a relativism of absolutisms. The way forward is through methodologies that can bring the normative and sociological derivative inferences of these absolutisms into meaningful dialogue. Dialogical standards of reliability and validity make that possible, or at least that is the claim of the ISM.

Dialogism will mean that 'truth' and 'objectivity' can guide relationships between psychology and religion but can never become finally attained goals. The triumphalism of any specific 'truth' and 'objectivity' would be inimical to dialogue. Dialogism can only advance 'truth' and 'objectivity' to the next and not to the final step of dialogue. One dialogical 'truth' and 'objectivity' will lead to the next and so on as one more complex 'truth' and 'objectivity' replaces another in a process that will be interminable but also productive.

Dialogue interpreted in this way will mean that any conclusions about the ISM will need to emphasize its commitment to inconclusion. Many will reject the ISM, and some may find many of its assumptions to be irrational. The ISM commitment to metaphysical theism may be especially irritating for some. The ISM should not offer triumphalist rejoinders that dismiss these or any other criticisms of its model of the relationship between psychology and religion. The appropriate response instead would be to advance the dialogue to the next step. Indeed, development of the ISM has been a decades-long processes in which earlier simplicities have given way to later complexities. Future dialogues will undoubtedly reveal ongoing needs for theoretical and methodological refinements. For example, is the word "triumphalism" appropriate for capturing the implications of monologisms? Is it insulting? Would some other term be better?

A useful conclusion for the ISM, therefore, might be a series of inconclusions that listed topics for possible future dialogues:

Perhaps at least some social scientists interested in the relationship between psychology and religion should renounce any implicit or explicit attempt to explain away one social rationality away based upon another. Incommensurability seems to require this.

Perhaps anti-psychological religionists should enter into dialogues about the dangers of ghettoization and the challenges of secularization. Perhaps they should have more faith in their own social rationality and its ability to function within the dynamics of scientific thinking. Or perhaps they should explain why such concerns about their ideological surround are misplaced.

Perhaps religious synthesizers should become more conscious of the intellectual challenges to faith since the time of William of Ockham. Perhaps they should work not only to integrate psychology with religion but to do so while also embracing methods that make it possible to reliably and validly critique psychology as well.

Perhaps social scientists interested in psychology and religion should make at least some effort to better understand the rationalities of public space. If there are reasons for more optimistic diagnoses of public space than those offered by the ISM, perhaps they can be made clear. Or to say the same thing differently, perhaps arguments can explain why triumphalisms, religious and otherwise, are not encouraging an atomization, fragmentation, and polarization that enervate public life and threaten the well-being of all. Cultural developments all across the planet suggest that this is a legitimate concern.

But perhaps the ISM diagnosis of public space is rational, or more precisely trans-rational. More proactively, therefore, perhaps social scientists regardless of their commitments to one or another ultimate standard can cooperate to develop provisional standards of dialogue in public space based upon shared derivative inferences. Perhaps the use of these provisional standards could work toward the construction of cooperation as an increasingly needed resource of social capital within and across cultures.

Perhaps dialogues of public space should be open to derivative inferences that include more and more of the affects that Nietzsche (1887/1967) used to define future objectivity: "There is only a perspective seeing, only a perspective 'knowing'; and the *more* affects we allow to speak about one thing, the *more* eyes, different eyes, we can use to observe one thing, the more complete will our 'concept' of this thing, our 'objectivity,' be" (p. 119). Perhaps an increased openness to diverse affects could enhance all dialogical rationalities.

Perhaps those derivative inferences should include the affects implied in the insight of Makhennet (2017) after her dialogues with jihadists, "If I've learned anything, it's this: a mother's screams over the body of her murdered child sound the same, no matter if she is black, brown, or white; Muslim, Jewish or Christian; Shia or Sunni. We will all be buried in the same ground" (p. 320). Perhaps, these tears and screams can also be extended to all victims of war and violence and fall on the same ground. Perhaps this same ground is essential to include in the common ground of public space. Perhaps this is sacred ground. Perhaps morality should never perish for as long as humanity may live. Perhaps we should take care of each other. Perhaps we should love each other.

Acknowledgements

Acknowledgement should be given to the endless array of dialogical partners who have influenced the ISM, including those who have been skeptical. My favorite negative reaction to the ISM occurred in a peer-review of a paper that led to rejection by one journal followed by a later acceptance elsewhere (Watson, Hood, and Morris 1985). This paper sought to offer an ideologically balanced assessment of relationships between religious orientations and empathy. The initial negative reviewer accused the author of giving comfort to 'brown shirts.' What this reviewer could not have known was that the author was and is a Quaker (Watson 2006). In other words, this critique implied that the paper was a product of Nazi Quakerism. It is almost impossible to imagine two perspectives that are more diametrically opposed than Nazism and Quakerism. Still, this was a wonderful comment, the kind of thing that makes you scratch your head and worry about the problems of social rationality in public space.

Many supportive dialogues have, of course, been essential to the development of the ISM. Nothing would have been possible without the love and help of my wife, Jackie. For more than 35 years, she made it possible for me to lose myself in research. Her patience and encouragement, her handling of practical life while I lost myself in idealism, have literally been *the* central contribution to the ISM research program. No words can express the magnitude of my gratitude.

Ralph Hood has been a miracle in my life. Before I came to the University of Tennessee at Chattanooga (UTC) four decades ago, I really did not think very deeply about the relationship between psychology and religion. Ralph made the importance of that relationship very clear. He began as a departmental colleague, and then a friend, role model, and indispensable dialogical partner. Ralph is not guilty of any imprecisions or outright mistakes of judgment in this monograph. He is, however, responsible for many of its strengths.

Research colleagues have made irreplaceable contributions. Over 20 years ago, Nima Ghorbani in Iran and I began a collaboration that eventually supplied critical insights for the ISM. Other invaluable international colleagues have included Ziasma Haneef Khan in Pakistan, Shanmukh Kamble in India, and Mustafa Tekke in Malaysia and then Turkey. In the United States, Ron Morris at UTC and Job Chen at UTC and then Clemson University have been wonderful friends and invaluable research collaborators as well.

Christian psychologists as friends and colleagues have supplied invaluable dialogical insights as well. Eric Johnson is, in my opinion, a true hero in the attempt to bring Christianity and psychology into meaningful dialogue. His work deserves much wider appreciation. Interactions with him and with our mutual friend and colleague Tim Sisemore, another profoundly important Christian psychologist, have left their positive indelible imprints on the ISM.

For four decades, UTC gave me a home where I could flourish intellectually. In recent years, Brian O'Leary served as a department head who made it possible for me to address what sometimes seemed to be overwhelming challenges. In the middle of a recent semester, for example, I was working on this overview of the ISM when doctors discovered that I had life-threatening medical conditions that necessitated immediate treatment and release from my teaching responsibilities. Suddenly, I confronted the pressure of trying to meet the conditions of a contract from Brill to complete this review of the ISM when the number of days left to me remained unclear. These circumstances eventually forced me into a reluctant retirement. In all this, Brian literally saved the day by making it possible for me to become a professor emeritus with an opportunity to work toward the completion of this monograph. I am deeply grateful.

Also, with regards to UTC, other past and previous UTC Psychology faculty and staff members have also supported my work in one way or another, with George Helton, Mike Biderman, Nicky Ozbek, and Angelique Cook deserving my special thanks. The appreciation that I owe to my UTC students defies description. I principally taught mostly freshmen taking Introductory Psychology and mostly juniors and seniors taking a social sciences seminar in the University Honors (UHON) Program. Both groups of students taught me a great deal about the diversity and complexity of social rationalities. Many insights associated with the ISM grew out of this UHON course. I am so very grateful to Greg O'Dea and Debbie Bell for this UHON opportunity.

Finally, the ISM would not have been possible without the spiritual home made available to me by Chattanooga Friends Meeting and by Quaker traditions more generally (Fox 1694/1985; Woolman 1774/1961). Chattanooga Friends have generally supported each other in ways that have helped me and everyone else within Meeting to pursue their own, often diverse personal visions of life as best as they could. Larry and Becky Ingle, in particular, have been there for me when I needed them the most. Larry also served as a role model of someone who could thoughtfully combine Quaker with academic commitments (e.g., Ingle 1994). Peter Cottingham, who is no longer with us, drifted in and out of Meeting over the years in his trips back and forth between Chattanooga and the UK. He shared stories of huddling with his mother in the London Underground as German bombs fell overhead during WWII. At the close of our silent Meeting for Worship, he would often whisper under his breath, "Thy will be done." Amen to that.

References

Abu-Raiya, Hisham. (2012). "Towards a Systematic Qura'nic Theory of Personality." *Mental Health, Religion & Culture* 15: 217–233. doi:10.1080/13674676.2011.640622.

Abu-Raiya, Hisham. (2014). "Western Psychology and Muslim Psychology in Dialogue: Comparisons between a Qura'nic Theory of Personality and Freud's and Jung's Ideas." *Journal of Religion and Health* 53: 326–338. doi:10.1007/s10943-012-9630-9.

Abu Raiya, Hisham, Kenneth I. Pargament, Annette Mahoney, and Catherine Stein. (2008). "A Psychological Measure of Islamic Religiousness: Development and Evidence for Reliability and Validity." *The International Journal for the Psychology of Religion* 18: 291–315. doi:10.1080/10508610802229270.

Altemeyer, Bob, and Bruce Hunsberger. (1992). "Authoritarianism, Religious Fundamentalism, Quest, and Prejudice." *The International Journal for the Psychology of Religion* 2: 113–133. doi:10.1207/s15327582ijpr0202_5.

Altemeyer, Bob, and Bruce Hunsberger. (2004). "A Revised Religious Fundamentalism Scale: The Short and Sweet of It." *The International Journal for the Psychology of Religion* 14: 47–54. doi:10.1207/s15327582ijpr1401_4.

Andrews, Benjamin, P. J. Watson, Zhuo J. Chen, and Ronald J. Morris. (2017). "Postmodernism, Positive Psychology, and Posttraumatic Growth within a Christian Ideological Surround." *Journal of Positive Psychology* 12: 489–500. doi:10.1080/17439760.2016.1228004.

Appleyard, Bryan. (1992). *Understanding the Present*. New York: Doubleday.

Baron, Reuben M., and David A. Kenny. (1986). "The Moderator-Mediator Variable Distinction in Social Psychological Research: Conceptual, Strategic, and Statistical

Considerations." *Journal of Personality and Social Psychology* 51: 1173–1182. doi:10.1037//0022-3514.51.6.1173.

Batson, Charles Daniel, Patricia Schoenrade, and W. Larry Ventis. (1993). *Religion and the Individual*. New York: Oxford University Press. doi:10.2307/1386643.

Berger, Peter. (1967). *The Scared Canopy*. Garden City, NY: Anchor Books.

Biddle, Mark E. (2005). *Missing the Mark*. Nashville, TN: Abingdon Press.

Boenig-Liptsin, Margo. (2015). "The Intermediary Case." In *Can We Survive Our Origins?*, edited by Pierpaola Antonello and Paul Gifford, pp. 267–273. East Lansing, MI: Michigan State University Press. doi:10.14321/j.ctt14bsoq3.18.

Brauer, Simon. (2018). "The Surprising Predictable Decline of Religion in the United States." *Journal for the Scientific Study of Religion* 57: 654–675. doi:10.1111/jssr.12551.

Budner, Stanley. (1962). "Intolerance of Ambiguity as a Personality Variable." *Journal of Personality* 30: 29–50. doi:10.1111/j.1467-6494.1962.tb02303.x.

Bufford, Rodger K., Timothy A. Sisemore, and Amanda M. Blackburn. (2017). "Dimensions of Grace: Factor Analysis of Three Grace Scales." *Psychology of Religion and Spirituality* 9: 56–69. doi:10.1037/rel0000064.

Buss, David M., and David P. Schmitt. (1993). "Sexual Strategies Theory: An Evolutionary Perspective on Human Mating." *Psychological Review* 100: 204–232. doi:10.1037//0033-295x.100.2.204.

Cavanaugh, William T. (2009). *The Myth of Religious Violence*. New York: Oxford University Press. doi:10.1086/656653.

Coe, John H., and Todd W. Hall. (2010). "A Transformational Psychology View." In *Psychology and Christianity: Five views* (2nd ed.), edited by Eric L. Johnson, pp. 199–226. Downers Grove, IL: IVP Academics.

Descartes, René. (1968). *Discourse on Method and Meditations on First Philosophy*. London: Penguin Books. (Original works published in 1637 and 1641.)

Dover, Hanan, Maureen Miner, and Martin Dowson. (2007). "The Nature and Structure of Muslim Religious Reflection." *Journal of Muslim Mental Health* 2: 189–210. doi:10.1080/15564900701614858.

Dumouchel, Paul. (2015). "Misrecognition of 'Misrecognition.'" In *Can We Survive Our Origins?*, edited by Pierpaola Antonello and Paul Gifford, pp. 273–279. East Lansing, MI: Michigan State University Press. doi:10.1080/0048721x.2016.1209035.

Dupuy, Jean-Pierre. (2015). "Nuclear Apocalypse: The Balance of Terror and Girardian 'Misrecognition.'" In *Can We Survive Our Origins?* edited by Pierpaola Antonello and Paul Gifford, pp. 253–266. East Lansing, MI: Michigan State University Press. doi:10.14321/j.ctt14bsoq3.17.

Duriez, Bart, Bart Soenens, and Dirk Hutsebaut. (2005). "Introducing the shortened Post-Critical Belief Scale." *Personality and Individual Differences* 38: 851–857. doi:10.1016/j.paid.2004.06.009.

Ellis, Albert. (1962). *Reason and Emotion in Psychotherapy*. Secaucus NJ: Citadel Press.

Ellis, Albert. (1980). "Psychotherapy and Atheistic Values: A Response to A. E. Bergin's 'Psychotherapy and Religious Values.'" *Journal of Consulting and Clinical Psychology* 48: 635–639. doi:10.1037//0022-006x.48.5.635.

Fox, George. (1985). *The Journal of George Fox*. Philadelphia, PA: Philadelphia Yearly Meeting of the Religious Society of Friends. (Original work published 1694.)

Francis, Leslie J., Abdullah Sahin, and Fahad Al-Failakawi. (2008). "Psychometric Properties of Two Islamic Measures among Young Adults in Kuwait: The Sahin-Francis Scale of Attitude toward Islam and the Sahin Index of Islamic Moral Values." *Journal of Muslim Mental Health* 3(1): 9–24. doi:10.1080/15564900802035201.

Freud, Sigmund. (1961a). *The Future of an Illusion*. New York, NY: W. W. Norton and Company. (Original work published in 1927.)

Freud, Sigmund. (1961b). *Civilization and Its Discontents*. New York, NY: W. W. Norton. (Original work published 1930.)

Freud, Sigmund. (1964). *New Introductory Lectures*. Standard edition (Vol. 22, pp. 3–182). London: Hogarth. (Original work published 1933.)

Freud, Sigmund. (1990). *The Ego and the Id*. New York: W. W. Norton & Company. (Original work published 1923.)

Fukuyama, Francis. (2006). *The End of History and the Last Man*. New York: Free Press.

Gaukroger, Stephen. (1995). *Descartes: An Intellectual Biography*. Oxford: Oxford University Press.

Gellner, Ernest. (1992). *Postmodernism, Reason and Religion*. London: Routledge.

Ghorbani, Nima, P. J. Watson, Naser Aghababaei, and Zhuo J. Chen. (2014). "Transliminality and Mystical Experience: Common Thread Hypothesis, Religious Commitment, and Psychological Adjustment in Iran." *Psychology of Religion and Spirituality* 6: 268–275. doi:10.1037/a0037432.

Ghorbani, Nima, P. J. Watson, Mahmood Amirbeigi, and Zhuo J. Chen. (2016). "Religious Schema within a Muslim Ideological Surround: Religious and Psychological Adjustment in Iran." *Archive for the Psychology of Religion* 38: 253–277. doi:10.1163/15736121-12341327.

Ghorbani, Nima, P. J. Watson, Mansureh Asadi, and Zhuo J. Chen. (2018). *Muslim Religion and Spirituality in Cadets: Further Evidence of Complexity and Diversity in Iranian Religious Commitments*. Manuscript submitted for publication.

Ghorbani, Nima, P. J. Watson, Zhuo J. Chen, and Hanan Dover. (2013). "Varieties of Openness in Tehran and Qom: Psychological and Religious Parallels of Faith and Intellect Oriented Islamic Religious Reflection." *Mental Health, Religion & Culture* 16: 123–137. doi:10.1080/13674676.2011.647809.

Ghorbani, Nima, P. J. Watson, Shiva Geranmayepour, and Zhuo J. Chen. (2013). "Analyzing the Spirituality of Muslim Experiential Religiousness: Relationships with Psychological Measures of Islamic Religiousness in Iran." *Archive for the Psychology of Religion* 35: 233–258. doi:10.1163/15736121-12341264.

Ghorbani, Nima, P. J. Watson, Shiva Geranmayepour, and Zhuo J. Chen. (2014a). "Measuring Muslim Spirituality: Relationships of Muslim Experiential Religiousness with Religious and Psychological Adjustment in Iran." *Journal of Muslim Mental Health* 8: 77–94. doi:10.3998/jmmh.10381607.0008.105.

Ghorbani, Nima, P. J. Watson, Shiva Geranmayepour, and Zhuo J. Chen. (2014b). "Muslim Experiential Religiousness: Relationships with Attitude toward Islam, Religious Reflection, and Basic Needs Satisfaction in Iranians." *Research in the Social Scientific Study of Religion* 25: 53–72. doi:10.1163/9789004272385_005.

Ghorbani, Nima, P. J. Watson, Hamid R. Gharibi, and Zhuo J. Chen. (2018). "Model of Muslim Religious Spirituality: Impact of Muslim Experiential Religiousness on Religious Orientations and Psychological Adjustment among Iranian Muslims." *Archive for the Psychology of Religion* 40: doi:10.1163/15736121-12341354.

Ghorbani, Nima, P. J. Watson, Hamed Kashanaki, and Zhuo J. Chen. (2017). "Diversity and Complexity of Religion and Spirituality in Iran: Relationships with Self-Compassion and Self-Forgiveness." *International Journal for the Psychology of Religion* 27: 157–171. doi:10.1080/10508619.2017.1340100.

Ghorbani, Nima, P. J. Watson, and Ziasma H. Khan. (2007). "Theoretical, Empirical, and Potential Ideological Dimensions of Using Western Conceptualizations to Measure Muslim Religious Commitments." *Journal of Muslim Mental Health* 2: 113–131. doi:10.1080/15564900701613041.

Ghorbani, Nima, P. J. Watson, Maryam Madani, and Zhuo J. Chen. (2016). "Muslim Experiential Religiousness: Spirituality Relationships with Psychological and Religious Adjustment in Iran." *Journal of Spirituality and Mental Health* 18: 300–315. doi:10.1080/19349637.2016.1162676.

Ghorbani, Nima, P. J. Watson, Fatemeh Rabiee, and Zhuo J. Chen. (2018). *Religious Fundamentalism in Iran: Religious and Psychological Adjustment within a Muslim Cultural Context*. Manuscript submitted for publication.

Ghorbani, Nima, P. J. Watson, Zoha Saeedi, Zhuo J. Chen, and Christopher F. Silver. (2012). "Religious Problem-Solving and the Complexity of Religious Rationality within an Iranian Muslim Ideological Surround." *Journal for the Scientific Study of Religion* 51: 656–675. doi:10.1111/j.1468-5906.2012.01686.x.

Ghorbani, Nima, P. J. Watson, Zahra Sarmast, and Zhuo J. Chen. (2018). "Post-critical Beliefs and Religious Reflection: Religious Openness Hypothesis in Iranian University and Islamic Seminary Students." *Journal of Empirical Theology* 31: 49–70. doi:10.1163/15709256-12341367.

Ghorbani, Nima, P. J. Watson, Kadijeh Shamohammadi, and Christopher J. L. Cunningham. (2009). "Post-critical Beliefs in Iran: Predicting Religious and Psychological Functioning." *Research in the Social Scientific Study of Religion* 20: 151–194. doi:10.1163/ej.9789004175624.i-334.50.

Ghorbani, Nima, P. J. Watson, Fazlollah Tavakoli, and Zhuo J. Chen. (2016). "Self-Control within a Muslim Ideological Surround: Empirical Translation Schemes and the Adjustment of Muslim Seminarians in Iran." *Research in the Social Scientific Study of Religion* 27: 68–93. doi:10.1163/9789004322035_005.

Ghorbani, Nima, P. J. Watson, Fazlollah Tavakoli, and Zhuo J. Chen. (2018). "Mindfulness within a Muslim Ideological Surround: Empirical Translation Schemes and Religious and Psychological Functioning of Islamic Seminarians in Iran." *Research in the Social Scientific Study of Religion* 29: 305–308. doi:10.1163/9789004382640_016.

Giddens, Anthony. (1990). *The Consequences of Modernity*. Stanford, CA: Stanford University Press.

Gifford, Paul. (2015). "Survival without Salvation?" In *Can We Survive Our Origins?*, edited by Pierpaola Antonello and Paul Gifford, pp. 279–284. East Lansing, MI: Michigan State University Press. doi:10.1080/0048721X.2016.1209035.

Girard, René. (1978). *Things Hidden since the Foundation of the World*. Stanford, CA: Stanford University Press.

Girard, René. (2010). *Battling to the End*. East Lansing, MI: Michigan State University.

Gorsuch, Richard L., and Susan E. McPherson. (1989). "Intrinsic/Extrinsic Measurement: I/E Revised and Single-Item Scales." *Journal for the Scientific Study of Religion* 28: 348–354. doi:10.2307/1386745.

Habermas, Jürgen. (1984). *The Theory of Communicative Action*. Vol. 1. Boston, MA: Beacon.

Hardin, Michael (ed.). (2015). *Reading the Bible with René Girard: Conversations with Steven E. Berry*. JDL Press.

Hart, David B. (2009). *Atheist Delusions*. New Haven, CT: Yale University Press.

Haven, Cynthia L. (2018). *The Evolution of Desire: A Life of René Girard*. East Lansing, MI: Michigan State University Press.

Hermans, Hubert J. M. and Harry J. G. Kempen. (1993). *The Dialogical Self*. San Diego, CA: Academic Press.

Hodge, David R. (2003). "The Intrinsic Spirituality Scale: A New Six-Item Instrument for Assessing the Salience of Spirituality as a Motivational Construct." *Journal of Social Service Research* 30: 41–61. doi:10.1300/J079v30n01_03.

Hunsberger, Bruce. (1996). "Religious Fundamentalism, Right-Wing Authoritarianism, and Hostility toward Homosexuals in Non-Christian Religious Groups." *The International Journal for the Psychology of Religion* 6: 39–49. doi: 10.1207/s15327582ijpr0601_5.

Hunter, James D. (1991). *Culture Wars*. New York: Basic Books.

Ingle, H. Larry. (1994). *First among Friends*. Oxford, UK: Oxford University Press.

Jalal, Ayesha. (2008). *Partisans of Allah*. Cambridge, MA: Harvard University Press.

Johnson, Eric L. (2007). *Foundations for Soul Care*. Downers Grove, IL: IVP Academic.

Jonason, Peter K. and Gregory D. Webster. (2010). "The Dirty Dozen: A Concise Measure of the Dark Triad." *Psychological Assessment* 22: 420–432. doi:10.1037/a0019265.

Jones, Alvin, and Rick Crandall. (1986). "Validation of a Short Index of Self-Actualization." *Personality and Social Psychology Bulletin* 12: 63–73. doi:10.1177/0146167286121007.

Jones, Stanton. (2010). "An Integration View." In *Psychology and Christianity: Five Views* (2nd ed.), edited by Eric L. Johnson, pp. 101–128. Downers Grove, IL: IVP Academics.

Kaltner, John. (2011). *Introducing the Qur'an for Today's Reader*. Minneapolis, MN: Fortress Press.

Kamble, Shanmukh V., P. J. Watson, Deepti B. Duggi, and Zhuo J. Chen. (2018). "Fundamentalism within an Indian Ideological Surround: Commitment to Religious Tradition Predicts Hindu Openness." *Research in the Social Scientific Study of Religion* 29: 329–351. doi:10.1163/9789004382640_017.

Kamble, Shanmukh V., P. J. Watson, Savitri Marigoudar, and Zhuo J. Chen. (2014). "Varieties of Openness and Religious Commitment in India: Relationships of Attitudes toward Hinduism, Hindu Religious Reflection, and Religious Schema." *Archive for the Psychology of Religion* 36: 172–198. doi:10.1163/15736121-12341283.

Kaufmann, Walter. (1974). *Nietzsche: Philosopher, Psychologist, Antichrist* (4th ed.). Princeton, NJ: Princeton University Press.

Khan, Ziasma H., P. J. Watson, Hafiza N. Ali, and Zhuo J. Chen. (Forthcoming). "Greater jihad of Society and Self: Religious and Psychological Implications in Pakistani Madrassa and University Students." *International Journal for the Psychology of Religion*. doi:10.1080/10508619.2018.1517016.

Khan, Ziasma H., P. J. Watson, and Zhuo J. Chen. (2016). "Muslim Spirituality, Religious Coping, and Reactions to Terrorism among Pakistani University Students." *Journal of Religion and Health* 55: 2086–2098. doi:10.1007/s10943-016-0263-2.

Khan, Ziasma H., P. J. Watson, and Zhuo J. Chen. (2018). "Religious Reflection in Pakistan: Further Evidence of Integration between Muslim Faith and Intellect." *Journal of Beliefs and Values* 39: 258–262. doi:10.1080/13617672.2017.1292725.

King, Martin L., Jr. (1963). "I have a dream...." Retrieved August 10, 2018, from https://www.archives.gov/files/press/exhibits/dream-speech.pdf.

Loewenthal, Kate M. (2013). "Religion, Spirituality, and Culture: Clarifying the Direction of Effects." In *APA Handbook of Psychology, Religion, and Spirituality (vol. 1): Context, Theory, and Research*, edited by Kenneth I. Pargament, Julie J. Exline and James W. Jones, pp. 239–255. Washington, DC: American Psychological Association. doi.org/10.1037/14045-013.

MacIntyre, Alasdair. (1978). *Against the Self-Images of the Age*. Notre Dame, IN: University of Notre Dame Press.

MacIntyre, Alasdair. (1988). *Whose Justice? Which Rationality?* Notre Dame, IN: University of Notre Dame Press.

MacIntyre, Alasdair. (1990). *Three Rival Versions of Moral Enquiry*. Notre Dame, IN: University of Notre Dame Press.

MacIntyre, Alasdair. (2009). *God, Philosophy, Universities*. London: Rowan and Littlefield Publishers.

Marler, Penny L. and C. Kirk Hadaway. (2002). "'Being Religious' or 'Being Spiritual' in America: A Zero-Sum Proposition?" *Journal for the Scientific Study of Religion* 41: 289–300. doi:10.1111/1468-5906.00117.

Maslow, Abraham. (1993). *The Farther Reaches of Human Nature*. New York: Arkana/Penguin. (Original work published 1971.)

Mekhennet, Souad. (2017). *I Was Told to Come Alone: My Journey behind the Lines of Jihad*. New York: Henry Holt and Company.

Myers, David G. (2010). "A Levels-of-Explanation View." In *Psychology and Christianity: Five Views* (2nd ed.), edited by Eric L. Johnson, pp. 49–78. Downers Grove, IL: IVP Academics.

Narramore, S. Bruce. (1984). *No Condemnation*. Grand Rapids: Zondervan.

Nasr, Seyyed H. (2002). *The Heart of Islam*. San Francisco, CA: HarperSanFrancisco.

Nietzsche, Friedrich. (1967). "On the Genealogy of Morals." In *On the Genealogy of Morals and ecce homo*, edited by Walter Kaufman, pp. 13–163. New York: Random House. (Original work published in 1887.)

Northcott, M. (2015). "Girard, Climate Change, and Apocalypse." In *Can We Survive Our Origins?*, edited by Pierpaola Antonello and Paul Gifford, pp. 287–309. East Lansing, MI: Michigan State University Press. doi:10.14321/j.ctt14bsoq3.18.

Pargament, Kenneth I. (2013). "Searching for the Sacred: Toward a Nonreductionistic Theory of Spirituality." In *APA Handbook of Psychology, Religion, and Spirituality (vol. 1): Context, Theory, and Research*, edited by Kenneth I. Pargament, Julie J. Exline and James W. Jones, pp. 257–273. Washington, DC: American Psychological Association. doi:10.1037/14045-014.

Pargament, Kenneth I., Margaret Feuille, and Donna Burdzy. (2011). "The Brief RCOPE: Current Psychometric Status of a Short Measure of Religious Coping." *Religions* 2: 51–76. doi:10.3390/rel2010051.

Pargament, Kenneth. I., Joseph Kennell, William Hathaway, Nancy Grevengoed, Jon Newman, and Wendy Jones. (1988). "Religion and the Problem-Solving Process: Three Styles of Coping." *Journal for the Scientific Study of Religion* 27: 90–104. doi:10.2307/1387404.

Placher, William C. (1994). *Narratives of a Vulnerable God*. Louisville, KY: Westminster John Knox Press.

Popper, Karl R. and John C. Eccles. (1983). *The Self and Its Brain*. New York, NY: Routledge.

Porpora, Douglas V. (2006). "Methodological Atheism, Methodological Agnosticism and Religious Experience." *Journal for the Theory of Social Behaviour* 36: 57–75. doi:10.1111/j.1468-5914.2006.00296.x.

Powlison, David. (2010). "A Biblical Counseling View." In *Psychology and Christianity: Five Views* (2nd ed.), edited by Eric L. Johnson, pp. 245–273. Downers Grove, IL: IVP Academics.

Pratto, Felicia, Jim Sidanius, Lisa M. Stallworth, and Bertram F. Malle. (1994). "Social Dominance Orientation: A Personality Variable Predicting Social and Political Attitudes." *Journal of Personality and Social Psychology* 67: 741–763. doi:10.1037//0022-3514.67.4.741.

Ramm, Bernard L. (1985). *Offense to Reason: A Theology of Sin*. San Francisco, CA: Harper and Row.

Roberts, Robert C. and P. J. Watson. (2010). "A Christian Psychology View." In *Psychology and Christianity: Five Views* (2nd ed.), edited by Eric L. Johnson, pp. 149–178. Downers Grove, IL: IVP Academics.

Rosenau, Pauline M. (1992). *Post-modernism and the Social Sciences*. Princeton, NJ: Princeton University Press.

Roth, Paul A. (1987). *Meaning and Method in the Social Sciences*. Ithaca, NY: Cornell University Press.

Sampson, Edward E. (1993). *Celebrating the Other: A Dialogical Account of Human Nature*. Boulder, CO: Westview Press.

Sandage, Steven J., Peter J. Jankowski, Sarah A. Crabtree, and Maria L. Schweer-Collins. (2017). "Calvinism, Gender Ideology, and Relational Spirituality: An Empirical Investigation of Worldview Differences." *Journal of Psychology and Theology* 45: 17–32. doi:10.1177/009164711704500102.

Sen, Ragini, Wolfgang Wagner, and Caroline Howarth. (2014). *Secularism and Religion in Multi-faith Societies: The Case of India*. Cham: Springer International Publishing. doi:http://dx.doi.org.proxy.lib.utc.edu/10.1007/978-3-319-01922-2.

Shostrum, E. L. (1974). *Manual for the Personal Orientation Inventory*. San Diego, CA: Educational and Industrial Testing Service.

Smith, Brewster. (1973). "On Self-Actualization: A Transambivalent Examination of a Focal Theme in Maslow's Psychology." *Journal of Humanistic Psychology* 13: 17–33. doi:10.1177/002216787301300203.

Smither, Robert, and Alireza Khorsandi. (2009). "The Implicit Personality Theory of Islam." *Psychology of Religion and Spirituality* 1: 81–96. doi:10.1037/a0015737.

Sorokin, Pitirim A. (1992). *The Crisis of Our Time*. Oxford: Oneworld Publications. (Original work published 1941.)

Stout, Jeffrey. (1988). *Ethics after Babel*. Boston: Beacon Press.

Streib, Heinz, Ralph W. Hood, Jr., and Constantin Klein. (2010). "The Religious Schema Scale: Construction and Initial Validation of a Quantitative Measure for Religious Styles." *International Journal for the Psychology of Religion* 20: 151–172. doi:10.1080/10508619.2010.481223.

Tangney, June P., Roy F. Baumeister, and Angie L. Boone. (2004). "High Self-Control Predicts Good Adjustment, less Pathology, Better Grades, and Interpersonal Success." *Journal of Personality* 72: 271–322. doi:10.1111/j.0022-3506.2004.00263.x.

Tarnas, Richard. (1991). *Passions of the Western Mind.* New York: Ballantine Books.

Taylor, Charles. (1989). *Sources of the Self.* Cambridge, MA: Harvard University Press.

Taylor, Charles. (2007). *A Secular Age.* Cambridge, MA: The Belknap Press.

Tekke, Mustafa, P. J. Watson, Nik A. Hirsham İsmail, and Zhuo J. Chen. (2015). "Muslim Religious Openness and *ilm*: Relationships with Islamic Religious Reflection, Religious Schema, and Religious Commitments in Malaysia." *Archive for the Psychology of Religion* 37: 295–320. doi:10.1163/15736121-12341313.

Thauberger, Patrick C., and Daniel Sydiaha-Symor, D. (1977). "The Relationship between an Avoidance of Existential Confrontation and Neuroticism: A Psychometric Test." *Journal of Humanistic Psychology* 17: 89–91. doi:10.1177/002216787701700109.

Toulmin, Stephen E. (1990). *Cosmopolis.* New York: Free Press.

Van der Lans, Jan M. (1987). "The Value of Sundén's Role-Theory Demonstrated and Tested with Respect to Religious Experiences in Meditation." *Journal for the Scientific Study of Religion* 26: 401–412. doi:10.2307/1386443.

Watson, P. J. (1993). "Apologetics and Ethnocentrism: Psychology and Religion within an Ideological Surround." *International Journal for the Psychology of Religion* 3: 1–20. doi:10.1207/s15327582ijpr0301_1.

Watson, P. J. (1998). "Girard and Integration: Desire, Violence, and the Mimesis of Christ as Foundation for Postmodernity." *Journal of Psychology and Theology* 26: 311–321. doi:10.1177/009164719802600401.

Watson, P. J. (2004). "After Postmodernism: Perspectivism, a Christian Epistemology of Love, and the Ideological Surround." *Journal of Psychology and Theology* 32: 248–261. doi:10.1177/009164710403200309.

Watson, P. J. (2006). "Friends of the Truth, Violence, and the Ideological Surround: Social Science as Meetings for Clearness." *Archive for the Psychology of Religion* 28: 123–132. doi:10.1163/008467206777832643.

Watson, P. J. (2008). "Faithful Translation and Postmodernism: Norms and Linguistic Relativity within a Christian Ideological Surround." *Edification: Journal of the Society for Christian Psychology* 2(1): 5–18. Retrieved November 29, 2018, from http://www.christianpsych.org/wp_scp/wp-content/uploads/edification-journal-21.pdf#page=4.

Watson, P. J. (2010). "Christian Rationality and the Postmodern Context: The Example of Rational-Emotive Therapy within a Christian Ideological Surround." *Edification: The Transdisciplinary Journal of Christian Psychology* 4(1): 64–74. Retrieved November 29, 2018, from http://www.christianpsych.org/wp_scp/wp-content/uploads/Edification-4.1.pdf#page=64.

Watson, P. J. (2011). "Whose Psychology? Which Rationality? Christian Psychology within an Ideological Surround after Postmodernism." *Journal of Psychology and Christianity* 30: 307–316. Retrieved on December 19, 2018, from https://www.researchgate.net/publication/281442553_Whose_Psychology_Which_Rationality_Christian_Psychology_within_an_Ideological_Surround_after_Postmodernism.

Watson, P. J. (2014). "Transition beyond Postmodernism: Pluralistic Culture, Incommensurable Rationalities, and Future Objectivity." *Review & Expositor* 111: 33–40. doi.org/10.1177/0034637313510480.

Watson, P. J., Zhou J. Chen, and Nima Ghorbani. (2014). "Extrinsic Cultural Religious Orientation: Analysis of an Iranian Measure in University Students in the United States." *Journal of Beliefs and Values* 35: 61–78. doi:10.1080/13617672.2014.884849.

Watson, P. J., Zhou J. Chen, Nima Ghorbani, and Meghdi Vartanian. (2015). "Religious Openness Hypothesis: I. Religious Reflection, Schemas, and Orientations within Religious Fundamentalist and Biblical Foundationalist Ideological Surrounds." *Journal of Psychology and Christianity* 34: 99–113. Retrieved December 11, 2018 from https://www.researchgate.net/profile/Paul_Watson4/publication/281294398_Religious_Openness_Hypothesis_I_Religious_Reflection_Schemas_and_Orientations_within_Religious_Fundamentalist_and_Biblical_Foundationalist_Ideological_Surrounds/links/55e09da308ae6abe6e897508.pdf.

Watson, P. J., Zhuo J. Chen, and Ralph W. Hood, Jr. (2011). "Biblical Foundationalism and Religious Reflection: Polarization of Faith and Intellect Oriented Epistemologies within a Christian Ideological Surround." *Journal of Psychology and Theology* 39: 111–121. doi:10.1177/009164711103900202.

Watson, P. J., Zhuo J. Chen, and Ronald J. Morris. (2014). "Varieties of Quest and the Religious Openness Hypothesis within Religious Fundamentalist and Biblical Foundationalist Ideological Surrounds." *Religions* 5: 1–20. doi:10.3390/rel5010001.

Watson, P. J., Zhuo J. Chen, and Ronald J. Morris. (2018). "Sanctification of Learning and Religious Openness: Contrasts across Religious Fundamentalist and Biblical Foundationalist Ideological Surrounds." *Research in the Social Scientific Study of Religion* 29: 352–376. doi:10.1163/9789004382640_018.

Watson, P. J., Zhuo J. Chen, Ronald J. Morris, and Nima Ghorbani. (2017). "Religious Problem-Solving Styles within an American Religious Ideological Surround." *Research in the Social Scientific Study of Religion* 28: 22–51. doi:10.1163/9789004348936_003.

Watson, P. J., Zhuo J. Chen, Ronald J. Morris, and Nima Ghorbani. (2018). "Religion within a Dark Triad Ideological Surround: Pluralistic Self as Dialogue across Private, Communal, and Public Space." *Research in the Social Scientific Study of Religion* 29: 377–400. doi:10.1163/9789004382640_019.

Watson, P. J., Zhuo J. Chen, Ronald J. Morris, and Erin Stephenson. (2015). "Religious Openness Hypothesis: III. Defense against Secularism within Fundamentalist and Biblical Foundationalist Ideological Surrounds." *Journal of Psychology and Christianity* 34: 125–140. Retrieved December 11, 2018 from https://www.researchgate .net/publication/281294655_Religious_Openness_Hypothesis_III_Defense_ against_Secularism_within_Fundamentalist_and_Biblical_Foundationalist_ Ideological_Surrounds.

Watson, P. J., Nima Ghorbani, Meghdi Vartanian, and Zhuo J. Chen. (2015). "Religious Openness Hypothesis: II. Religious Reflection and Orientations, Mystical Experience, and Psychological Openness of Christians in Iran." *Journal of Psychology and Christianity* 34: 114–124. Retrieved December 11, 2018 from https://www. researchgate.net/publication/281294403_Religious_Openness_Hypothesis_II_ Religious_Reflection_and_Orientations_Mystical_Experience_and_Psychological_ Openness_of_Christians_in_Iran.

Watson, P. J., Ralph W. Hood, Jr., and Ronald J. Morris. (1985). "Dimensions of Religiosity and Empathy." *Journal of Psychology and Christianity* 4(3): 73–85. Retrieved December 11, 2018 from https://www.researchgate.net/publication/ 232432379_Dimensions_of_Religiosity_and_Empathy.

Watson, P. J., Ralph W. Hood, Jr., and Ronald J. Morris. (1988). "Existential Confrontation and Religiosity." *Counseling and Values* 33: 47–54. doi:10.1002/j.2161-007x.1988 .tb00735.x.

Watson, P. J., J. Trevor Milliron, Ronald J. Morris, and Ralph W. Hood, Jr. (1994). "Religion and Rationality: II. Comparative Analysis of Rational-Emotive and Intrinsically Religious Rationalities." *Journal of Psychology and Christianity* 13: 373–384. Retrieved on December 19, 2018 from https://www.researchgate.net/publication/232526470_ Religion_and_rationality_II_Comparative_analysis_of_rational-emotive_and_ intrinsically_religious_irrationalities.

Watson, P. J., J. Trevor Milliron, Ronald J. Morris, and Ralph W. Hood, Jr. (1995). "Religion and the Self as Text: Toward a Christian Translation of Self-Actualization." *Journal of Psychology and Theology* 23: 180–189. doi:10.1177/009164719502300304.

Watson, P. J., and Ronald J. Morris. (2006). "Intolerance of Ambiguity within a Religious Ideological Surround: Christian Translations and Relationships with Religious Orientation, Need for Cognition, and Uncertainty Response." *Archive for the Psychology of Religion* 28: 81–101. doi:10.1163/008467206777832634.

Watson, P. J., and Ronald J. Morris. (2008). "Self-Control within a Christian Ideological Surround." *Edification: Journal of the Society for Christian Psychology* 2(2): 62–72. Retrieved on November 29, 2018 from http://www.christianpsych.org/wp_scp/wp-content/uploads/edification-22.pdf#page=62.

Watson, P. J., Ronald J. Morris, and Ralph W. Hood, Jr. (1987). "Antireligious Humanistic Values, Guilt, and Self-Esteem." *Journal for the Scientific Study of Religion* 26: 535–546. doi:10.2307/1387103.

Watson, P. J., Ronald J. Morris, and Ralph W. Hood, Jr. (1988a). "Sin and Self-Functioning, Part 1: Grace, Guilt, and Self-Consciousness." *Journal of Psychology and Theology* 16: 254–269. doi:10.1177/009164718801600305.

Watson, P. J., Ronald J. Morris, and Ralph W. Hood, Jr. (1988b). "Sin and Self-Functioning, Part 2: Grace, Guilt, and Psychological Adjustment." *Journal of Psychology and Theology* 16: 270–281. doi:10.1177/009164718801600306.

Watson, P. J., Ronald J. Morris, and Ralph W. Hood, Jr. (1989). "Sin and Self-Functioning, Part 5: Antireligious Humanistic Values, Individualism, and the Community." *Journal of Psychology and Theology* 17: 157–172. doi:10.1177/009164718901700210.

Watson, P. J., Ronald J. Morris, Taylor Loy, Michael B. Hamrick, and Sheldon Grizzle. (2007). "Beliefs about Sin: Adaptive Implications in Relationships with Religious Orientation, Self-Esteem, and Measures of the Narcissistic, Depressed and Anxious Self." *Edification: Journal of the Society for Christian Psychology* 1: 57–67. Retrieved December 1, 2018, from http://www.christianpsych.org/wp scp/wp-content/uploads/edification-journal-113.pdf#page=57.

Watson, P. J., Benjamin S. Reagan, Zhuo J. Chen, and Ronald J. Morris. (Forthcoming). "Xenophilia and the Religious Openness Hypothesis: Love of the 'Stranger' within Religious Fundamentalist and Biblical Foundationalist Ideological Surrounds." *Journal of Psychology and Theology*. doi:10.1177/0091647118807184.

Watson, P. J., Pauline Sawyers, Ronald J. Morris, Mark L. Carpenter, Rachael S. Jimenez, Katherine A. Jonas, and David L. Robinson. (2003). "Reanalysis within a Christian Ideological Surround: Relationships of Intrinsic Religious Orientation with Fundamentalism and Right-Wing Authoritarianism." *Journal of Psychology and Theology* 31: 315–328. doi:10.1177/009164710303100402.

Williamson, W. Paul, Ralph W. Hood, Jr., Aneeq Ahmad, Mahmood Sadiq, and Peter C. Hill. (2010). "The Intratextual Fundamentalism Scale: Cross-cultural Application, Validity Evidence, and Relationship with Religious Orientation and the Big 5 Factor Markers." *Mental Health, Religion & Culture* 13: 721–747. doi:10.1080/13674670802643047.

Woolman, John. (1961). *The Journal of John Woolman*. Secaucus, NJ: The Citadel Press. (Original work published in 1774.)

Wulff, David M. (1997). *Psychology of Religion: Classic and Contemporary*. (Second ed.). New York: John Wiley & Sons.

Zinnbauer, Brian J., Kenneth I. Pargament, Brenda Cole, Mark S. Rye, Eric M. Butter, Timothy G. Belavich, and Jill L. Kadar. (1997). "Religion and Spirituality: Unfuzzying the Fuzzy." *Journal for the Scientific Study of Religion* 36: 549–564. doi:10.2307/1387689.